RUBBER
STAMPING
with Other Crafts

RUBBER STAMPING

with Other Crafts

Lynne Garner

Guild of Master Craftsman Publications Ltd

First published 1999 by
Guild of Master Craftsman Publications Ltd,
166 High Street, Lewes,
East Sussex BN7 1XU

ISBN 1 86108 109 X

Photographer: Paul Jarvis
Editor: Cathy Lowne
Designer: Kate Buxton
Typefaces: Barbedor and Latin
Colour origination by Viscan Graphics (Singapore)
Printed and bound by Kyodo Printing (Singapore) under the supervision of MRM Graphics,
Winslow, Buckinghamshire, UK

10 9 8 7 6 5 4 3 2 1

CONTENTS

Dedication

This book is dedicated to the memory of
my father, Gordon Henry Garner. It was not finished
until it was Garnerized!

Acknowledgements

I would like to thank my close family and friends for
all their support, Paul and Scott for putting up with
one of those 'author types' during the photo shoot and,
especially, my fiancé Jon, who must have proofread
this book more times than he or I can count. I would
like to thank the following people for the kind supply
of items used in this book and their invaluable help:

Michael Bossom of Arts Encaustic, without whose help
and advice I would not have been able to complete the
encaustic art chapter; Roger Button of Creative Stamping
at Express; Hazel and Linda Chambers of S for Stamps;
Andy Charman of The Guild of Master Craftsman
Publications Ltd who held my hand from start to finish;
Pam Fenton of Edding UK Ltd; Mike Gutteridge of
Personal Impressions; Janice Halliwell of Craft Creations;
Jennie Hulme of The Stamp Connection for her help and
support; Sue Jones of Harvey Baker Design Ltd; Lloyd
Mathews of StoneCraft®, whose brainstorming sessions
were invaluable; Michelle Powell of Rubber Stampede;
Caroline Rawcliffe of CaroLines; Barbara Santerelli of
Clarity Stamps for designing some wonderful stamps;
Nicci Simmonds of Stamps 'n' Stencils of Hitchin
for her help and advice (and allowing me
to use one of her ideas).

INTRODUCTION

When I was first introduced to rubber stamps my first reaction was: Oh, great, I can make some really nice hand-made cards with these. What to do with the rubber stamps once I had made my cards was a mystery. I then saw an article where someone had stamped onto an index box and then coloured in the designs. What a great idea! I then realised that there were so many other crafts that could be mixed with rubber stamping that the world was now full of endless possibilities. I could use my rubber stamps to decorate items for my home, my family, my friends and perhaps, if I ever got around to it, for myself.

I have found while teaching and writing that people tend not to dabble with only one craft, but like to try out as many as they can, and this book will hopefully fuel that desire. Mixing rubber stamping with other techniques seems the next obvious progression with this wonderful, versatile craft.

Trying new craft skills can be daunting, but just remember that nothing is a failure or a mistake. Everything you do is an experiment; some experiments work first time while others, hopefully, will work next time. Nothing is so bad that it cannot be tried again. If you do not succeed the first time, have fun with your crafting and the results may even surprise you.

Within the pages of this book I explore and discuss the basics of 10 fascinating crafts, all of which are then mixed with rubber stamping in 20 projects ranging from jewellery to household items. My hope is that they inspire you to continue to experiment with rubber stamping and to have fun with this wonderfully addictive craft. My philosophy is that if it stands still long enough you can stamp it and if it does not stand still long enough pin it down and stamp it anyway!

CHAPTER 1

THREE-DIMENSIONAL
DECOUPAGE

Technique

Three-dimensional decoupage is the art of creating a 3-D image from a number of identical prints. It is one of those craft techniques that you tend to marvel at before you understand it but, once you have grasped the basics, it is a craft that becomes highly addictive.

Rubber stamps are ideal for this technique, which requires between four and six identical images (or more if you want) to build up the picture. With a rubber stamp you can make as many copies as you require, and it is certainly cheaper than buying five or more identical prints. This craft not only provides the satisfaction of creating a wonderful image, but also offers the challenge of finding a picture that will translate into three dimensions. You will find yourself looking at rubber stamps in a new light, wondering if you can use them for 3-D decoupage.

Once mastered, the techniques are simple yet effective. All the tools needed are easy to obtain and, on the whole, inexpensive. For example, if you wish to frame your finished design you will probably find that the frame is the most expensive item you buy. However, expensive purchases are not necessary: this technique can also be used to decorate many household items such as trinket boxes and storage jars, as well as enabling you to save money with projects like your own beautiful, personalized cards.

Materials *and equipment*

- Rubber stamp
- Black ink pad
- Thick paper or thin card (large enough to stamp the image at least five times)
- Small decoupage scissors (nail scissors or a craft knife will do)
- Build-up glue (decoupage silicone glue) or double-sided sticky pads
- Teaspoon
- Pin
- Foam mat (a parchment craft mat or a mouse mat would be ideal)
- Water-soluble pencils
- Dry glue stick
- Surface to work on (when cutting out with scissors a tray is ideal)
- Cold glaze (formulated especially for decoupage and available from good hobby shops)

Method

Make sure that the stamp you have chosen is suitable for this technique. Choose an image that consists of distinct layers, where one piece of the design appears to sit behind another piece. Try to see the image as if you were seeing it in real life and judge which elements would be farthest away from you and which would be nearer. I prefer to do my cutting with decoupage scissors which have a slight curve to the blade.

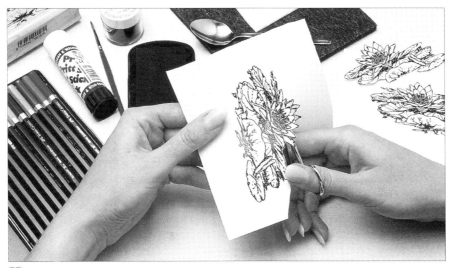

Step 3

STEP 1   Stamp as many copies of the image as you need. For a greetings card, I would suggest no more than four layers (the card might not stand up if you use more). When making a framed picture you can use six or more layers to create a 3-D effect. Colour each copy.

STEP 2   If you want the image to go in a frame or card, cut out one copy of the entire image together with a border if you want one. This will be your background base print, so put it to one side. You do not have to include a border, but can just cut out the entire image.

STEP 3   Now cut out the next layer using a second print, leaving out sections of the image that appear to be farther back or behind the elements you are cutting out.

◩ *Step 4*

◩ *Step 5*

STEP 4 Continue with this process until you have cut out as many layers as required. Each layer will become smaller and you will probably have small pieces in the foreground layers. Keep the layers neatly laid out in order.

STEP 5 Now assemble the image. It is up to you whether you use build-up glue or double-sided sticky pads, but when gluing remember that the bigger the blob, the bigger the gap between the layers. Place each layer exactly over the same part of the last layer, in order to make the 3-D effect. If any glue is visible when the image is complete, rub it off gently with your finger when it is dry. If you prefer to use double-sided sticky pads then they can be cut to the size required (see Tips on page 9).

STEP 6 Protect the image with a coat of cold glaze.

Adding interest

CURLING

To give a more natural effect to petals, leaves or even limbs, use the back of a teaspoon to curl the top layer slightly. Place the section you wish to curve face down and work the back of the spoon in a gentle circular motion from the centre of the image to the outer edges. If the image curls too much, do not worry: it will soon flatten out when stuck into place. Only shape the final layers of your image.

PINPRICKING

To create more interest (perhaps in a flower centre) you can pinprick the surface of the final image before you attach it. For a smooth effect, push the pin through the image from the front to the back; for a textured effect push the pin through from the back to the front. Experiment with different-sized pins and the direction in which you prick the paper: you will be amazed at the interesting effects you can achieve with this simple technique.

UNEVEN LAYERING

Another way to add interest is to make part of the last layer stand out. You can build up just one side of the layer, with the other side glued directly to the surface of the previous layer or, for example, if you have an image of a curved item like a flowerpot, build up just the centre of the last layer by placing the glue or double-sided sticky pad in the middle and sticking the edges to the previous layer.

FEATHERING

Images that include animals with fur or prickles or rough-edged plants look more natural if these edges are uneven. To do this, snip into the edge and 'feather' it in order to ensure that there are no straight edges which will make the image look 'odd'. Slowly cut into the edge of the image in the correct direction for how the fur or prickles lie. If this is done carefully the cut section will curl slightly.

 *Tips*

- Always work layer-by-layer, starting at the back.

- Apply the glue or sticky pads as close to the edge as possible so that the paper does not curl up too much.

- If you use build-up glue then use a special decoupage silicone glue. You can use bathroom sealant, although I find this tends to be too oily. The sealant used for fish tanks is another alternative. Apply the glue to the reverse of the image as if you were icing a cake. Hold the tube 1mm (1/32in) above the print and squeeze gently, pulling away so that the line of glue is the required height. If you find this too difficult then put the glue onto a cocktail stick and then trail it into position.

- Cut the double-sided sticky pads into 3mm (1/8in) wide strips leaving the protective paper in place. Removing the paper from one side, stick enough bits of pad to the reverse of the image for the layer to sit evenly. Take off the rest of the protective paper and stick this layer to the one below. When an image contains a lot of elements, number the pieces as you go lightly on the reverse with a pencil.

- If you stamp on thin paper, mount it on thin card first. When stamping on card or using it as a mount, ensure that it is not too thick or you will have problems cutting it later.

- To improve the finished image, colour in the cut edges. You can match the medium you used to colour the image with: pencils, felt-tip pens or watercolours.

- Hang pictures away from direct sunlight or the colours will fade and the varnish will crack.

- If the image is for a card, use no more than four layers. Any more layers than this will make the card difficult to post without damaging it, and you may have problems getting it to stand up.

Framed picture

This image is ideal for the bathroom or toilet and will match most decors with its vibrant mix of colours. It is easy to produce and making your own set of identical prints saves you money.

Materials **and equipment**

- Underwater scene rubber stamp by S for Stamps (catalogue no: F1703L)
- Three pieces of A4 thin, cream card
- Black pigment ink stamp pad
- Black embossing powder
- Fine artist's brush
- Heat source (embossing heat gun, toaster, etc.)
- Water-soluble pencils
- Small container for water
- Scissors, or a craft knife and cutting mat
- Silicone build-up glue or double-sided sticky pads
- Embossing mat
- Teaspoon
- Masking tape
- Shadow box picture frame to fit

Method

STEP 1   Stamp the image six times onto the A4 card. Emboss each image with the black embossing powder as you go. If you do not emboss the image, the ink might run when you use the water-soluble pencils.

STEP 2   Using the water-soluble pencils, colour in the image. To save time and unnecessary work, just colour in the sections that you will be cutting out later.

STEP 3   Allow the colours to dry thoroughly and then cut out the sections. Mark each piece on the reverse lightly with a pencil to ensure that you do not lose track of which piece is which, and place them to one side, in order.

STEP 4   To begin building the image, start with the 'base' image and build the layers up one at a time. When you come to the last layers, or pieces, curl them gently with the back of a teaspoon.

STEP 5   Once all the sections are fixed into place, mount the completed decoupage in the shadow box and seal the back with masking tape.

Step 1

Step 2

Step 4

Greetings card

Each year we send thousands of cards for all manner of occasions and it is sometimes almost impossible to find an appropriate card. This card is ideal for keeping tucked away for just such an emergency. It can be sent as a Get Well or birthday card, or just serve as a notelet.

Materials *and equipment*

- Water Lily rubber stamp by Personal Impressions (catalogue no: 171P)
- Two pieces of good quality, white A4 paper
- Black pigment ink stamp pad
- Black embossing powder
- Fine artist's brush
- Heat source (embossing heat gun, toaster, etc.)
- Water-soluble pencils or watercolour paint
- Small container for water
- Decoupage scissors, or a sharp craft knife and cutting mat
- Silicone build-up glue or double-sided sticky pads
- Embossing mat
- Teaspoon
- Dry glue stick
- Pre-cut aperture card to fit image

Method

STEP 1 Stamp the image onto the paper five times, embossing each one as you go. If you do not use embossing powder the image might bleed when you colour it in with water-soluble pencils or watercolours.

STEP 2 Colour in the image. In order to save work just colour in the sections that will show on each layer.

STEP 3 Allow the images to dry completely. If they have buckled slightly place them beneath some heavy books for 15 to 20 minutes. Cut out the sections: first a complete image for the background, then the next layer that you feel would bring the image forward. Continue in this way until all the images are cut out. Mark each piece on the reverse lightly with a pencil to ensure that you do not lose track of which piece is which, and place them to one side, in order.

STEP 4 Mount the base image into the aperture card using the dry glue stick. When you are using an aperture card you do not have to keep the image within the aperture; sometimes you can create real impact by allowing it to burst out of the aperture. Now build the image up one layer at a time. When you come to the last layer, you can curl some of the pieces gently with the back of the teaspoon. You could also add extra interest by using uneven layering on the top layer.

Step 1

Step 2

Step 4

13

CHAPTER 2

VICTORIAN
DECOUPAGE

Technique

This decorative technique dates back centuries and was the pastime of the wealthy until with the invention of cheap printed images the Victorians turned it into an art form that could be practised by all classes. They used all kinds of images from cherubs to bowls of fruit to decorate every type of object imaginable. Today it is still a cheap option for decorating and renovating any item, whether big or small. When using the rubber stamp as the basis for your image, you can match any item with any room.

You can stamp as many images as you require, allowing you to transform not just an object but a complete room if you wish. The equipment needed is cheap and easy to get hold of: you may even find that most, if not all, of it is hidden around the house.

Materials
and equipment

- Paints suitable for the item you wish to decorate. If you are using anything other than water-based products you will need suitable cleaning fluids
- Rubber stamp/s
- Dye ink pad
- Paper (plain white or coloured)
- Pens, pencils (or another colouring medium)
- Small scissors, or a craft knife and cutting mat
- Water-soluble PVA glue
- Fine-grade sandpaper
- Medium-sized artist's brush
- Item to decorate
- Old jam jar
- Blu-tack
- Varnish suitable for the item you wish to decorate

Method

STEP 1 Ensure that the item you are decorating is both dirt free and dry, and remove any parts that are likely to get in the way while you are working (e.g. large handles or clasps).

STEP 2 Paint or varnish the item you are decorating.

STEP 3 While the item is drying you can work on the stamp designs. Stamp copies of your chosen image onto paper, with a couple of extras in case of accidents, then colour them in or leave them plain if you prefer. Once all the images are coloured, cut them out.

Step 3

STEP 4 Once the item to be decorated is completely dry, you can work out the position of the images. Attach a small piece of Blu-tack to the back of each image and press it into place. Work in this manner until you are happy with the layout of the images. You can lay the pieces so that they stand alone or overlap, as suits your design.

Step 4

STEP 5 Make a solution of water-soluble PVA glue and water in the jar (two parts glue to one part water).

STEP 6 Remove one of the images and carefully peel away the Blu-tack. Coat the back of the image with the glue-and-water solution. Lay the image back into position and gently smooth out any air bubbles with your fingers.

STEP 7 Once the image is in the correct position and you are sure there are no air bubbles, cover it with a layer of the glue-and-water solution to ensure that the image does not bleed into the varnish later. Repeat this process until all the images are in position, and allow the glue to dry completely.

STEP 8 You can now varnish the item. You will need to apply several coats of varnish to ensure a hard-wearing, smooth finish. Allow each coat to dry before the next is applied and sand the dried varnish after every couple of layers. The more coats of varnish you apply the better the final finish will be.

Step 6

Step 8

Tips

- Trial-size pots of emulsion paint, available from most DIY stores, are ideal for decorating small items.

- If you wish to age the images you have chosen, soak them in a solution of cold tea for a few minutes. Achieving the desired colour is a question of trial and error, so you may wish to experiment in advance. Allow them to dry thoroughly.

- If you do not have water-soluble pencils, you can use water-based felt-tip pens in the same way.

- If you find that you are getting brushmarks in your varnish, try using a spray varnish. This works best if you apply several thin coats, but you must use it in a well-ventilated room.

- Some inks are prone to run, so stamp your image and brush it with a mixture of PVA and water. If your ink still runs, change to another make or emboss the image using a pigment ink.

Safety

- When using chemicals always read the labels carefully and ensure that you use them in a well-ventilated room if necessary. Cover yourself and your work surfaces in case of accidents, and keep chemicals in a safe, secure place when they are not in use.

PROJECT 1

Black and silver trinket box

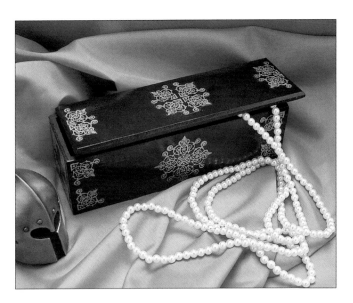

Once you master the art of making patterns with rubber stamps, this trinket box is simple and fun to make. This box has a real Gothic feel about it, but you could go for another feel entirely by simply changing the decoupage pattern. The box is suitable for a variety of uses and look great in many rooms of the house.

Materials *and equipment*

- Clever Corner rubber stamp from Clarity Stamps
- Black A4 paper
- Small scissors, or a craft knife and cutting mat
- Small household paintbrush and artist's brush
- Blank trinket box to decorate
- Black emulsion paint
- Embossing pigment ink pad
- Silver embossing powder
- Blu-tack
- Water-soluble PVA glue
- Fine-grade sandpaper
- Old jam jar
- Varnish suitable for the item being decorated
- Piece of cloth or tissue paper
- Masking tape
- Newspaper to cover work surface

Method

Step 2

Step 3

Step 4

STEP 1 Sand the wooden blank lightly if required, then remove any dust by wiping it gently with a cloth or tissue paper.

STEP 2 Paint the outside of the box with the black emulsion paint. If you do not want the paint to splash inside or underneath the box cover these areas with masking tape. Allow the paint to dry completely. If required, apply a second coat and allow it to dry.

STEP 3 While the paint is drying, stamp the images using the embossing pigment ink and silver embossing powder. Once the images have been embossed, carefully cut around each one with scissors or a craft knife.

STEP 4 Make up a solution of PVA glue and water in the jam jar. When the black paint is dry, begin to place the images onto the box. Cover the back of an image with the PVA glue-and-water mixture. Place it onto the box as accurately as possible and smooth it into the right position, working any air bubbles out with your fingers. Once you are pleased with the position, cover the front of the image with the PVA glue-and-water solution. Repeat for the other pieces of paper.

STEP 5 Allow to dry completely. Complete the box by applying several coats of varnish. Sand lightly after every couple of coats to improve the finish. The more coats of varnish you apply the better the finish and the more hard-wearing the final box will be.

✦ PROJECT 2

Desktop clock

Never let time slip by again with this fun desktop clock. It combines a functional timepiece with stylish black-and-white decoupage. It is simple to make and takes no time at all to complete.

Materials and equipment

- Blank clock kit (wooden clock, glue and sandpaper) by Harvey Baker designs Ltd
- White emulsion paint
- Small household paintbrush
- White A4 paper
- Black dye ink pad
- Small scissors
- Water-soluble PVA glue
- Small jam jar
- Small artist's brush
- Blu-tack
- Rubber stamps by Clarity Stamps
- Clear matt spray varnish

Method

⬖ *Step 1*

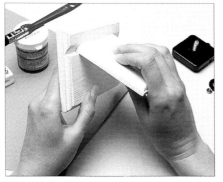

⬖ *Step 4*

⬖ *Step 8*

STEP 1   Sand the clock blank with the sandpaper provided in the kit to remove all of the rough edges.

STEP 2   Paint the wooden blank with at least two coats of the white emulsion paint, not forgetting to paint the back of the clock face. Allow the paint to dry.

STEP 3   Stamp the watch image several times on to the white A4 paper. When the ink is dry, carefully cut out each image with a craft knife or scissors.

STEP 4   Stick the clock face into position according to the instructions and allow the glue to set.

STEP 5   Using the Blu-tack to stick them down temporarily, experiment with where you would like to position the images on the clock.

STEP 6   Once you are happy with the position of the images, start to stick them into place using the PVA glue mixed with a little water. Smooth the images out with your fingers to remove any air bubbles. Cover the front of each image with the glue-and-water mix to create a barrier between the varnish and the black ink.

STEP 7   Apply several coats of spray varnish to create a good hard-wearing finish.

STEP 8   Once the varnish is completely dry, put the drawing pins into place (as shown on the instructions for the clock) and mount the clock movement.

CHAPTER 3

ENCAUSTIC
PAINTING

Technique

Encaustic art, or wax painting, is the art of creating images using coloured wax and an iron. Wax painting is not a new craft: examples that date back to Roman times are in existence. The Romans created wax pictures using similar techniques, although they did not have the benefit of thermostat-controlled irons or the range of coloured waxes available today.

To set yourself up is relatively cheap and, once you have the basic items, it is just a question of keeping a good stock of coloured waxes.

Rubber stamping and encaustic art blend together naturally. Although wax painting takes a little time to master, with a little practice you can soon make an image; the images shown on the next few pages can be produced easily and quickly using a few simple tools. Even if you have never painted before, you will soon be amazing yourself with your own artistic ability.

Materials
and equipment

- Encaustic iron
- Encaustic painting card (this is specially coated to make it non-absorbent)
- Encaustic wax (various colours, as well as clear)
- Rubber stamp
- Black dye ink pad
- Dry glue stick (for mounting the finished work)
- Newspaper (to cover your work surface)
- Scribing tool
- Tissue paper
- Wax sealer
- Small artist's brush

Method

STEP 1 Create large areas, such as hills, sky or lakes using the front curve of the base plate. Load one half of the base plate with wax and smooth the iron across the card in a sweeping motion. When creating hills, put the wax on the left side if you are right-handed, and on the right side if you are left-handed.

STEP 2 For such effects as an undersea background, smooth the iron across the card. Coat the entire base plate of the iron with coloured wax and lay the card flat on your work surface. Hold down one corner of the card with the tip of a finger and smooth the iron from one end of the card to the other. Do not 'iron' the card; let the iron float over the surface and the streaks will form naturally. Let the wax 'talk to you'; do not try to control the wax.

STEP 3 Dabbing is used to create foliage or coral. As you pull the iron away from the card air rushes in under the iron and creates the effect. Pick up the card and place your fingers underneath it to avoid getting iron marks. Now, holding the iron at an angle, bring the card into contact with the base plate. Do not let the card touch the edge of the iron or you will get marks and the foliage will look less natural. However, if you want to use the iron's edge to create abstract designs then leave the card flat on the work surface.

Step 1

Step 2

Step 3

STEP 4 Use the tip of the iron to create small, well-defined images, such as birds in flight. Pick up a small amount of wax on just the tip of the iron and just touch it to the card and flick it out and up to make the first wing. Repeat the process, but flick the tip in the other direction to complete a bird in flight. Dragonflies and flowers can also be created in this way, as can grass, bamboo and fencing.

STEP 5 By using the edge of the iron you can create blades of grass or seaweed. Experiment with this technique to create grass blades of different widths by changing the way you hold and move the iron.

STEP 6 A scribing tool allows you to remove a little of the wax to reveal the card beneath and to create paths, stars and birds quickly and simply. Just scratch the wax gently, then rub lightly with a tissue to remove the loose wax.

⬚⬚ Step 5

⬚⬚ Step 6

 *Tips*

- If you cannot find an encaustic iron a travel iron willl work just as well as long as it has no holes in the base.

- Set the iron on a very low heat, because you will be adding the wax straight onto the base plate. Hold the iron upside down so that you can smooth the wax onto the base plate without it running off. If the wax becomes very runny or smokes, the iron is too hot. The wax should melt on the base plate, look thick and run only slowly.

- It is better to use plenty of clear wax with a little colour. It is much easier to add a little colour to an area of a picture than to take it away.

- To start with do not plan a picture, but let it evolve. Floating images such as sea horses and dolphins are easier to begin with. All you have to do is supply an environment for them, not a firm surface. The ability to plan pictures will come with practice.

- A dye ink pad must be used for this type of stamping as a pigment ink will never dry on the specially coated card. It is best to stamp a small number of cards first and put them to one side to allow them to dry completely before you start painting. To dry them quickly, place a piece of tissue over the images and smooth them gently with a cool iron.

- If you wish to protect the surface of the image, coat it with wax sealer. Brush it on, ensuring that the strokes all run in the same direction.

- Always work from the middle to the outer edge or from the top to the bottom when adding details. This means that you do not have to worry about what is below the area you are working on.

- To clean the iron between pictures, cover the base plate with clear wax and wipe it clean with a tissue. Repeat this process once or twice until no more colour is picked up.

FRAMED PICTURE

The dolphin rubber stamp used to create this framed picture lends itself well to being teamed with wax painting. Once you have mastered the technique of wax painting, you could make yourself a set of these images, each with a different feel. They are a great way of cheering any wall and are sure to be the centre of attention when you have company.

Materials *and equipment*

- Encaustic iron
- A6 encaustic painting card
- Encaustic wax (light blue, green, dark blue, maroon and clear)
- Dolphin rubber stamp from Arts Encaustic
- Black dye ink pad
- Newspaper (to cover your work surface)
- Scribing tool
- Tissue paper
- Wax sealer
- Medium artist's brush
- Card mount to fit the image and frame
- Dry glue stick
- Tape
- Frame

Method

STEP 1 Stamp the image twice (slightly overlapping) onto the card using a fast-drying ink. Put to one side to allow the ink to dry completely. Before painting over the stamped image, hold it to the light at an angle to ensure the ink is fully dry.

STEP 2 Coat the base plate of your iron with the clear wax. Add the background colours to the clear wax.

STEP 3 Starting at one end of the card, smooth the iron across and repeat this process until you are happy with the coverage. Do not 'iron' the card, but let the iron float across it. Do not try to smooth out the streaks; use the shapes the wax makes.

STEP 4 Pick up the card and support it by placing your fingers under it. Dab the card with the iron to make the coral design around the image.

Tip

If you find that part of the stamped image does not come out, load a small artist's brush with a little ink from the pad and cover over any sections that have been missed.

Step 1

Step 2

Step 3

🔳 *Step 5*

STEP 5 To create a feeling of depth, add a few strands of seaweed by using the edge of the iron loaded with a little green. To hide the bottom of the seaweed, dab a little green and maroon across the lower image.

STEP 6 Using the scribing tool, remove the wax from the stomach of the dolphins so that the two animals are no longer part of the background but seem to be swimming through it.

STEP 7 Using a soft tissue, shine the completed image. Apply the wax sealer to the whole image, always brushing in the same direction.

STEP 8 Fix the image into an aperture card mount with the dry glue stick, then mount and tape it into your chosen frame.

PROJECT 2

Greetings cards

These simple-to-make, mystical images will bring a smile to the lucky person who receives one. Both cards are ideal for a variety of occasions. The colour schemes can easily be changed to create a completely different feel, perhaps using the recipient's favourite colours. The more you play with this technique, the more possibilities will open themselves up to you.

Materials
and equipment

- Encaustic iron (or travel iron without steam holes)
- A6 encaustic painting card
- Encaustic wax (blue, green, maroon and clear, or your own choice of colours)
- Rubber stamp: small castle or fairy
- Black dye ink pad
- Tissue paper
- Medium artist's brush
- Arts Encaustic wax sealer
- A5 pre-folded card
- Pre-cut card frame
- A5 coloured paper to match the card
- Dry glue stick
- Craft knife and cutting mat, or scissors

Method

STEP 1 Cut the piece of A6 encaustic card in half and stamp the image about one-third up from the bottom using the dye ink pad. Allow the image to dry.

STEP 2 Load the iron with the clear wax, covering the base plate completely, then add the blue, green and maroon waxes to create the background.

STEP 3 Place the card lengthways, so that the stamped image is on its side, and smooth the iron from one side to the other until the whole card is covered. Repeat, but lift the iron a little so that you get streaks. Clean the iron with the clear wax and some tissue.

STEP 4 Turn the card the right way up and the iron so that it is sideways onto the card. Smooth the iron across the bottom of the image to create ground for the castle or fairy to stand on.

Step 1

Step 3

Step 5

Step 7

STEP 5   Pick up the card and add some foliage in the foreground by dabbing the iron. This will give the castle a landscape to fit into, and the fairy somewhere to stand.

STEP 6   Once you have finished the image, shine the wax with a small piece of tissue. Apply wax sealer over the entire surface of the image, ensuring that all brush strokes run in the same direction. Allow to dry.

STEP 7   Centre the image onto one face of the pre-folded card and stick it down with the dry glue stick. Then lower onto it the pre-cut card frame.

STEP 8   Put an insert into the card using the piece of A5 paper (trim 2–3mm (about ⅛in) from the sides, then fold in half and stick it inside the finished card, making sure that the margin is the same all round).

CHAPTER 4

STONE-CUTTING

Technique

Most people might feel that this craft is beyond them, but it is far easier than one might expect. I must admit that when I was first introduced to stone-cutting I was a little sceptical, but within minutes I realised how easy it is: if you can cut card then you can cut stone. All it takes is a little patience and practice. It is far easier than it looks, and you will be amazed at the items you are soon able to make, ranging from jewellery to drinks coasters and other items for your home.

Many of the items used for this craft are available from most good hobby/craft shops or your local DIY store. You may even find most of the basic tools hidden around the house. So your biggest expense (and it is not really that expensive) is the stone itself. I have used packs of three sheets of stone by StoneCraft®. These come in a range of colours and are available from larger hobby retail outlets. The stone is soft sandstone. It is easy to work with and can be shaped as desired.

Materials
and equipment

- Stone sheets, pre-cut and boxed (available from StoneCraft®)
- Old toothbrush
- Pencil
- Hand-held nippers or tile cutters
- Small baking tray (to catch off-cuts as you work)
- Flat, stable work surface
- Newspaper (to cover your work surface)
- Hand-held metal file (large enough to file stone)
- Hand drill (*not* electric)
- Large nail
- Good-quality PVA glue

Method

STEP 1 Wash the stone thoroughly in water, using the toothbrush to remove any dust. Allow it to dry naturally.

STEP 2 Once the stone is dry, decide on the shape you want it to be and mark this on the stone with the pencil. This mark indicates the finished size.

STEP 3 Cut the stone down to almost the right size with a large nail and a pencil. Score the back of the stone with the nail, then place the score directly over the pencil with the score line facing upwards. Push the stone down on both sides of the pencil and it should break along the score line.

STEP 4 Decide where you want to start cutting. Hold the stone correctly: grip it with your index and middle fingers underneath and your thumb on top, directly opposite where you wish to make the first cut. To cut across the stone, place the tile cutters on the edge where you wish to make the break and apply pressure.

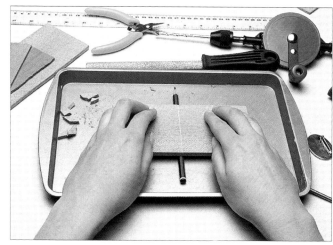

Step 3

Step 4

STEP 5 To cut out your shape, place the cutters on the pencil mark and apply pressure to them. Work around the shape, nibbling small sections at a time.

STEP 6 When you have shaped the piece, smooth down any rough edges with the metal file. Always work from the front to ensure an even shape. Check periodically to make sure that you are not taking off too much.

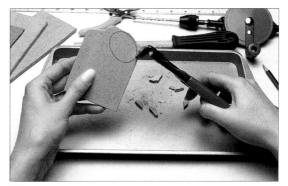

Step 5

Step 6

Safety

- When working with sharp tools make sure that you are holding them correctly and that your fingers are out of harm's way. Children must always be supervised by an adult.

- When drilling stone, always use a hand drill, not an electric drill. Work slowly, and stop regularly to clear away debris as it builds up.

- If you are worried about stone chippings flying up into your face, you should wear goggles. However, if you take care these should not be necessary.

 *Tips*

- Keep a vacuum cleaner handy to pick up the dust as you work.

- Work over a small baking tray to catch any small pieces of stone and dust as they fall.

- If you do not have very strong hands, use tile cutters.

- Make a mark on the back of the stone so that you can be sure of working from the front.

- Choose the correct stone to suit each project. For example, use 3mm (⅛in) stone for the jewellery and the 6–9mm (¼–⅜in) stone for the wall sconces project.

- Cut the piece out slightly larger than required. Rather than cutting away the extra few millimetres, use the file to create the size and shape you want.

- Until you have had enough practice to work with confidence, 'nibble' at the edges with the cutters rather than cutting large sections off at a time. Work slowly, in small sections and you will be less likely to make mistakes.

- When embossing on stone, use a pigment ink and work on a heat-resistant surface, because the stone will get very hot. Always allow the stone to cool completely before you pick it up; it can get hot enough to burn your fingers.

- Avoid solid stamps when embossing, as the embossing powder tends to bubble when heated, and try to use small-grained embossing powders as these give a better finish.

- Stick pieces of stone together or mount the stone into jewellery findings with a good-quality PVA glue. Dust the piece thoroughly to ensure that you get a good join. Try not to use too much glue or it will ooze out of the gap and spoil the look.

- When fixing the stone into a metal brooch, earring or ring backing, score the metal lightly with the nail to give the glue something to fix itself to.

- Remember that you are working with a natural material, so the colour will vary between boxes and sometimes between sheets of stone in the same box.

Pair of wall sconces

Candles have been a source of light for thousands of years and hold a fascination for everyone. Images of the sun and moon also hold a fascination and, when teamed with the age-old material of stone, create a wonderfully practical and decorative item for the home. These sconces also make accidents less likely as they ensure that the candles are up out of harm's way.

- Two packs of StoneCraft® stone (6–9mm (¼–⅜in) thickness)
- Old toothbrush
- Pencil
- Hand-held nippers or tile cutters
- Small baking tray or lap tray
- Flat, stable work surface
- Newspaper (to cover your work surface)
- Metal file
- Hand drill (*not* electric)
- Rubber stamps by Clarity Stamps
- Pigment ink pad
- White embossing powder
- Good-quality PVA glue
- Heat source for embossing

Materials *and equipment*

Method

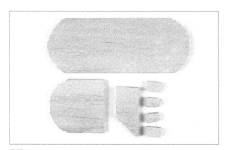
Step 2

Step 3

Step 4

Step 5

STEP 1   Clean all the pieces thoroughly with the old toothbrush and allow them to dry completely.

STEP 2   For *each* sconce, cut the stone to the required shapes following the diagram on page 44: make a back section, a shelf section, a third piece to serve as a shelf support and four small candle supports that attach to the top of the shelf.

STEP 3   Mark and drill – with a hand drill – a hole centred horizontally in the back section (roughly where the cross is on the diagram). This will enable you to hang up the sconce. Dust all the pieces thoroughly.

STEP 4   Now stamp the sun on the front of one back section, and the moon on the other, with the pigment ink. Sprinkle the ink with embossing powder and heat it, keeping your hands away from the stone. Allow the stone to cool.

STEP 5   Mark in pencil on each section the positions of the other pieces. Using good-quality PVA glue, stick the sconce together as follows: lay the back section face up on the work surface and stick the shelf section onto it at 90°. Then stick the shelf support into the angle under the shelf. Support this assembly and allow it to dry.

STEP 6   When the glue has set, stick the four candle supports towards the outer edge of the top of the shelf.

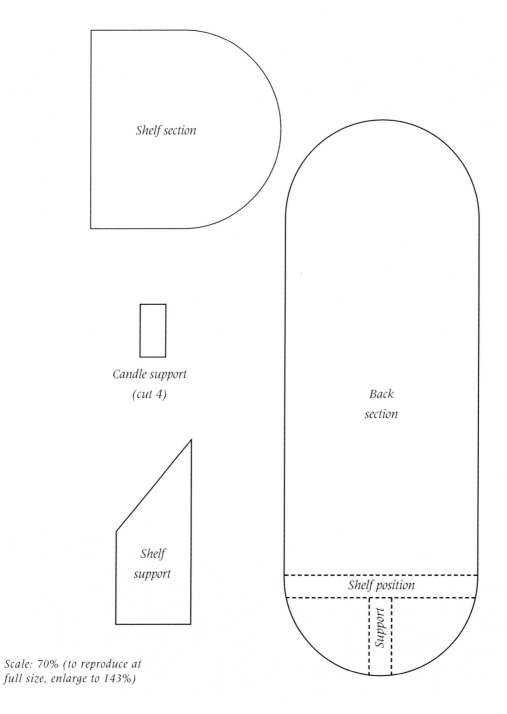

Shelf section

Candle support
(cut 4)

Shelf
support

Back
section

Shelf position

Support

Scale: 70% (to reproduce at
full size, enlarge to 143%)

PROJECT 2

Jewellery set

T he Celtic motif for this set of earrings, choker and brooch tones well with the feel and look of the stone used. The Celts are perhaps best known for their large stone crosses and carvings made on natural stone. So why not bring the stone and the Celtic design into the modern world and team them up to make simple but stylish jewellery?

- Stone (3mm (⅛in) thick, available from StoneCraft® in a variety of colours)
- Old toothbrush
- Hand-held nippers or tile cutters
- Small baking tray (to catch off-cuts)
- Flat, stable work surface
- Newspaper (to cover your work surface)
- Metal file
- Scrap paper
- Small scissors
- Large nail
- Pencil
- Good-quality all-purpose glue
- Rubber stamp by S for Stamps (no: A3160(S))
- Burgundy Fabrico ink pad
- Jewellery findings (earring backs, one brooch backing, one silver-tone claw, one silver-tone jump ring, a length of black cord and one clasp)
- Plaid Royal Coat Dimensional Magic

Materials
and equipment

Method

STEP 1 Wash the stone thoroughly and allow it to dry naturally.

STEP 2 While the stone is drying, make a paper template as follows: stamp the design onto the scrap paper and carefully draw a line about 2–3mm (approx. ⅛in) outside the exact line of the stamp. Cut out this template, ensuring that it is symmetrical.

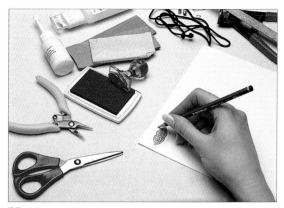

◱◲ *Step 2*

STEP 3 For each of the four items, place the template onto the clean, dry stone and draw around it.

STEP 4 Stamp the image into the centre of the pencil outline.

STEP 5 To separate the piece from the rest of the stone so that it is easier to work, score a straight line across the piece of stone with the large nail and break it over a pencil.

◱◲ *Step 4*

STEP 6 Use the tile cutters to nibble away small sections of stone using the pencilled line as your guide.

STEP 7 With the metal file, smooth the stone down to the required shape. Work from the front to ensure that the shape remains symmetrical.

STEP 8 Once you have the shape you require, highlight the stamped image with the Dimensional Magic. Then put the project to one side and allow it to dry.

◱◲ *Step 8*

TO COMPLETE THE EARRINGS

Apply a small dab of glue to the back of both pieces of stone and stick the backs into place. Place the earrings face down and allow the glue to set.

Sticking the backs into place

TO COMPLETE THE BROOCH

Glue the brooch finding into place, put it to one side, face down, and leave it to set.

Gluing the brooch

TO COMPLETE THE CHOKER

Apply a dab of glue to one of the points of the stone. Press the silver-tone clasp around the tip and allow the glue to set. Place a small silver-tone circle into the top of the cap and close it using a pair of pliers. Thread the black cord through the loop. Attach a silver-tone clasp to each end of the black cord to complete the choker.

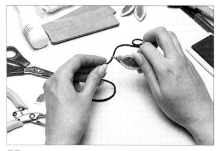

Threading the cord

Tips

- If you have problems stamping the design into the middle of the pencil line, stamp the image first then draw the shape around it.
- Tap the metal file into the baking tray occasionally so that its surface does not become clogged.
- This design can be altered by using embossing powder rather than the Dimensional Magic.
- The pencil mark should be used to show the finished size. Cut slightly outside this mark, then file down to achieve the correct size.

CHAPTER 5

TIE-DYE

Technique

Tie-dyeing is a method of adding colour and interest to fabric by creating a barrier between parts of the fabric and a cold-water dye to make patterns. Many different items can be used as a barrier, ranging from string to clothes pegs, and different patterns can be achieved simply by binding the fabric in different ways. Tie-dyeing can be done either before or after an item is made up. More than one colour can be used if the design requires it.

In this section I will discuss the basic method for creating tie-dye using string or elastic bands. Once you have mastered this technique you can explore and experiment with other forms of tie-dyeing (using stones, clothes pegs, bulldog clips and so on to create different patterns).

⧉ *Materials*
and equipment

- Cotton fabric or any item you wish
- String or elastic bands
- Scissors
- Cold-water dye/cold-water dye fixer
- Salt (refer to the instructions on the dye packet)
- Plastic bowl
- Protective rubber gloves
- Measuring jug

⧉ *Tips*

- To create a lighter area in the middle of the circle, bind a stone or marble inside the tip of the fabric cone.

- Always use natural fabrics rather than synthetics, because they take dye more easily. If using natural fabric, buy a little more than is required to allow for shrinkage.

- If you only want part of the item to take dye of one colour, just submerge that part and agitate it very gently from time to time.

Method

STEP 1   Always pre-wash the item to be dyed to remove the dressing and to ensure that it does not shrink later. If possible leave the item damp.

STEP 2   To create circles on your fabric, pinch a piece of fabric with one hand and pull it between the thumb and forefinger of the other hand to create a cone of fabric. Starting about 2.5–3cm (1–1½in) from the point of the fabric, tie the string tightly around the cone. Continue to wrap the string around the fabric tightly, working away from the tip. Tie off the string. If you prefer, you can use elastic bands as shown. Create more circles all over the fabric to be dyed.

STEP 3   Mix up the cold-water dye, salt and fixer in the plastic bowl according to the manufacturer's instructions. Place the item in the dye and allow it to soak for the correct length of time given, agitating the cloth regularly to ensure that all of it is submerged.

STEP 4   Once the dye has taken, remove the item from the dye-bath and rinse it until it no longer runs colour. Allow the item to dry naturally and remove the string or elastic bands carefully. Iron out the creases.

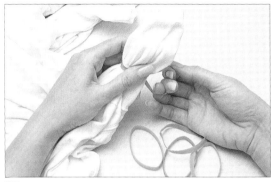

Step 2

Step 3

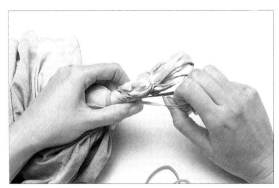

Step 4

PROJECT 1

Scarf

This scarf is ideal for teaming with all manner of items and it will be useful whatever the weather or time of year. It is also so cheap to make that you can easily make more than one, changing the colours to suit your mood and your wardrobe.

Materials and equipment

- Lightweight cotton fabric (50 x 150cm (18 x 60in))
- String or elastic bands
- Scissors
- Purple cold-water dye
- Salt
- Cold-water dye fixer
- Plastic bowl
- Protective gloves
- Cotton thread
- Sewing machine and basic sewing equipment
- Iron
- Scrap paper
- Fabrico ink pad (in a colour to tone with the purple dye)
- Rubber stamps by S for Stamps (catalogue nos: C1802(S), C1803(S) and C1816(S))

Method

STEP 1 Pre-wash the fabric and allow it to dry.

◈ *Step 2*

STEP 2 Remove the selvage (the tightly woven edge of the fabric) to avoid warping later.

◈ *Step 3*

STEP 3 To ensure that the fabric does not fray, turn the edges over twice, iron them, and then sew them down.

STEP 4 Bind, dye, fix the dye, then rinse and dry the fabric (see page 51). Remove the string, iron the fabric to remove the creases and lay it out onto a covered work surface.

STEP 5 Stamp the images several times onto scrap paper and cut them out roughly. Place them onto the fabric to work out your design.

Step 6

STEP 6 Once you are happy with the design, stamp each image, ensuring that the stamps have a good covering of ink.

STEP 7 Fix the ink by ironing it.

Tips

- Use natural cotton thread to sew the edges so it too will take up the dye.

- Always fix the dye with fixer and salt according to the manufacturer's instructions, as this will stop the colour bleeding if the fabric gets wet.

PROJECT 2
T-shirt

This fun T-shirt is suitable for all ages and both sexes and creates a one-off item from a basic white garment. If blue is not the colour for you, then simply choose another colour from the huge range of dyes available. This T-shirt is sure to become a firm favourite and when it has been worn to death can easily be created again (although, however hard you try, you will never get two exactly the same).

- Plain white cotton T-shirt
- Thick rubber bands
- Scissors
- Blue cold-water dye/cold-water dye fixer
- Salt
- Plastic bowl
- Protective gloves
- Measuring jug
- Iron
- Scrap paper
- Perspex-mounted rubber stamp from Clarity Stamps
- Pins
- Fabrico ink pad (blue)

Materials
and equipment

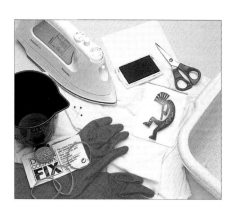

Method

STEP 1 Pre-wash the T-shirt and leave it damp.

STEP 2 Bind and dye the T-shirt (see page 51). When it has taken the dye, rinse it out under cold water until the colour no longer runs.

STEP 3 Allow the T-shirt to dry naturally and when it is completely dry remove the rubber bands and iron out the creases. Lay it out onto a covered work surface.

STEP 4 Decide how many copies of the image you want around the bottom of the T-shirt and how far apart they need to be. Use the Perspex mount of the stamp as a guide; once you have the position right, mark it with pins placed either side of the mount.

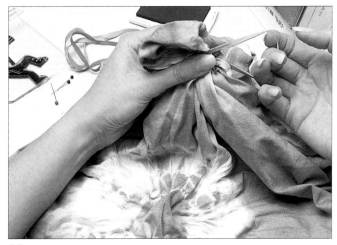

Step 3

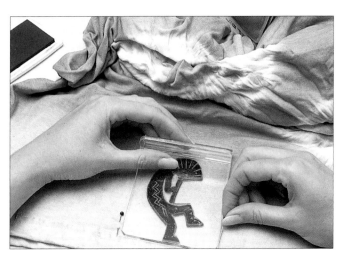

Step 4

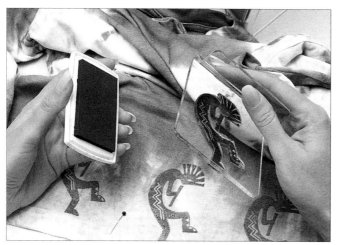

◩ *Step 6*

◩ *Step 7*

STEP 5 Place a piece of paper between the front and back of the T-shirt to prevent the ink from seeping through when you are stamping the design.

STEP 6 Stamp the images onto the bottom of the T-shirt, working your way from front to back and using the pins as guides.

STEP 7 Fix the ink with an iron, according to the manufacturer's instructions.

CHAPTER 6

STENCILLING

Technique

Stencilling has become very popular over the last few years: it is the art of creating an image on any surface by pushing colour pigment through a cut-out motif. You can alter the look of many items, ranging from walls to boxes, with just a brush or sponge and a stencil. Stencils with a wide range of motifs are available from many good hobby and craft shops as well as many DIY stores. Alternatively, if you are unable to find a stencil that you like, it is easy to make your own.

In this section I will cover stencilling with both brushes and sponges as well as showing how to make your own stencils. Specialist stencilling paints are now available, but you can also improvise using many sorts of paints, inks and gilt-creams. None of the alternatives is as good as the stencilling paints, but you can adjust your technique to suit the paint being used.

Materials and equipment

- Clear acetate film (available from most good hobby/craft shops)
- Chosen design
- Cutting mat
- Tracing paper
- Pencil
- Good-quality craft knife
- Masking tape
- Stencil (shop-bought if you have not made your own)
- Specialist stencilling paint or emulsion paint
- Stencilling brush (for solid stencilling paint) or sponge (for emulsion paint)
- Item to stencil
- Kitchen paper towels or similar
- Damp tissue paper or sponge for cleaning stencil
- Repositioning spray or masking tape

Method

TO MAKE YOUR OWN STENCIL

STEP 1 Place your chosen design under a piece of tracing paper and trace the design through. At this point decide where the 'bridges' of the stencil will be. These are the 2–3mm (about ⅛in) pieces that hold internal bits of the stencil (such as the 'holes' in letters) in place; they break the image into smaller sections and allow you to create lines within the design.

Step 1

STEP 2 Once the design is complete, place it onto your cutting mat. Put the acetate film over the top and fix it into position with the masking tape

STEP 3 Carefully cut out each section, taking care not to cut into the bridges as this will weaken the finished stencil. Remove all of the cut-out sections. Peel off the masking tape and take your completed stencil off the cutting mat.

Step 3

STENCILLING WITH SOLID STENCILLING PAINT

STEP 1 Fix the stencil onto the item using either repositioning spray or masking tape.

STEP 2 Tap the stencil brush onto the surface of the solid paint in order to pick up some of the pigment.

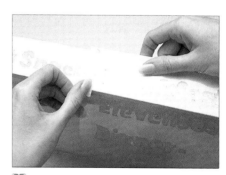

Step 1

STEP 3 Wipe the brush on a piece of dry tissue to ensure that you do not have to much paint on the tip.

61

STEP 4 Dab the brush gently in small circles over the area you wish to colour. You can create different effects by applying the paint in different ways, for example, to make the highlights on fruit, leave some areas of the stencil untouched.

Step 4

STENCILLING WITH A SPONGE AND EMULSION PAINT

STEP 1 Fix the stencil in position using repositioning spray or masking tape.

STEP 2 Dip the sponge into the paint. To ensure that there is not too much paint on the sponge, dab the excess onto some scrap paper. You need to remove as much paint as possible, but not all of it; judging the correct amount will come with practice.

Step 2

STEP 3 Dab the sponge over the stencil until the desired effect is achieved. If you need to put more paint onto the sponge, dip it back into the paint and then dab the excess on the scrap paper as before.

STEP 4 Lift the stencil off carefully and, if necessary, wipe the paint from it to avoid any risk of smudging. Repeat the above process until the stencilling is complete, making sure that you do not touch any of the wet images.

Step 4

 *Tips*

- Use a stencilling brush for specialist stencil paints and a sponge (with small, even holes) for emulsion paints.

- Practise on a piece of scrap paper before starting any project, so you can get the feel of the materials.

- You need not limit yourself to one solid colour; experiment with different ones. You can blend them by sponging one colour over another (start with the lighter colours) or graduate them by overlapping similar colours that you have placed next to each other.

- If you do not have repositioning spray or masking tape, you can use Blu-tack to keep the stencil in place. Take a small piece of Blu-tack and roll it into a thin sausage shape. Fix this to the underside of the stencil and press it down firmly onto your item. This method is not really suited to stencilling with emulsion paints, however, because the liquid might leak under the stencil.

- You can stencil on card or paper with a sponge and a pigment or dye ink pad. These inks shouldn't bleed under the stencil.

- Do not be afraid to 'play' with this technique; experiment with coverage and colour. For instance, you can leave areas in the centre of the image uncovered to make highlights and create depth, or bleed and overlay colours to achieve a softer effect. You will soon find a look that suits what you wish to do.

- If, when you varnish your completed projects, you find there are brush marks on the surface, try using spray varnish instead.

❈ PROJECT 1

Wastepaper bin

The bin is an essential everyday object that we all take for granted. Why not change all that by making yours stylish and unique? It will look more attractive than most bins that you can buy and you can make it to suit your own decor.

- Acetate film
- Craft knife and cutting mat
- Stencil designs
- Masking tape
- Blank wooden wastepaper bin
- Light green emulsion paint
- Dark green emulsion paint
- Medium-sized household paintbrush
- Small sponge
- Leaf rubber stamps by Personal Impressions (catalogue nos: 370F, 371F and 373F)
- Green verdigris embossing powder
- Embossing ink pad or pigment ink pad
- Heat source (embossing heat gun, etc)
- Varnish (clear matt or gloss)
- Small artist's brush
- Piece of cloth or tissue paper
- Newspaper (to cover your work surface)

Materials
and equipment

Method

STEP 1 Mask off the interior and base of the bin with the masking tape.

STEP 2 Now paint the outside of the bin with the light green paint and allow it to dry. If required, paint a second coat.

STEP 3 While the paint is drying, trace the leaf stencil designs onto the acetate, and cut these out using the craft knife.

Step 1

Enlarge or reduce this template to suit the size of the project.

STEP 4 When the paint is dry, stencil the leaf design randomly over the bin using the sponge and the dark green paint. Some of the leaves should bend around the corners and run off the edges. Leave enough space between the leaves to add stamps later. Work on one side at a time, allowing each to dry before stencilling the next.

STEP 5 Using the small artist's brush, touch up any bleeding or smudges with the dark green paint. To add interest, paint in veins on the stencilled leaves.

STEP 6 When all four sides are stencilled and the paint is absolutely dry, stamp and emboss the smaller leaves in between the stencilled designs. The stencilled paint must be completely dry or the embossing powder might stick to it.

STEP 7 Once all four sides have been stamped and embossed, apply several coats of clear varnish.

Step 5

Step 6

PROJECT 2

Tray

A tray is one of those little items that are essential around the home, whether you are having a TV dinner or treating your loved one to breakfast in bed. This one is both decorative and functional, and is easy to decorate using stencilling paint and a few stamps. You could even make a set of them: a different-coloured one for each member of the family.

Materials and equipment

- Blank wooden tray
- Trial-size pot of almond white emulsion paint
- Blue solid stencil paint
- Stencil brush (12mm (½in))
- Masking tape
- Acetate film
- Craft knife and cutting mat
- Photocopy of wording template
- Rubber stamps by Creative Stamping (catalogue nos: ASR469A, ASR468B and ASR467D)
- Blue ink stamp pad (Fabrico is great for this)
- Pencil
- Ruler
- Medium-sized household paintbrush
- Small artist's brush
- Cloth rag
- Matt spray varnish
- Newspaper (to cover the work surface)

Method

STEP 1 Before painting the tray, sand down all the surfaces, then remove any dust with a cloth.

STEP 2 Stick masking tape all round the outer edge of the base of the tray, then paint the top and sides of the tray with the white emulsion paint. Allow it to dry. Apply a second coat if necessary and allow to dry before proceeding.

STEP 3 While the paint is drying trace the lettering onto the acetate. Then cut out your stencil from the acetate with the craft knife. Using a cutting mat will protect your work surface and help to stop the knife slipping. To keep the acetate in position, fix it in place with the masking tape.

STEP 4 Once the paint is dry and you have cut out the stencil lettering, fix the stencil in place on the outside edge of the tray with the masking tape. Load the stencil brush with paint, wipe off the excess and dab the brush gently over the lettering in small circular motions. Work around the tray in this fashion until all four sides are complete.

Step 2

STEP 5 Touch up any smudges with white paint.

STEP 6 Now mark the positions for the teapot stamps. Make a light pencil mark halfway along each side of the tray. Then make a mark halfway along the correct edge of the teapot stamp so that you can align this mark with those on the tray.

STEP 7 Use the position for the teapot stamp to work out the correct places for the teacups. Align the marks on the teapot stamp with those on the tray and pencil lightly along the sides of the stamp. The first teacup stamps butt up to this line. On the long side of the tray, put the teacup stamp into position and make a pencil mark down the other side of the stamp to show the position for the next teacup.

STEP 8 Position the teaspoon stamps correctly by aligning pencil marks made in the centre of the short sides with lines drawn from the corners of the tray.

Step 9

STEP 9 Stamp all the images carefully with the blue ink pad. Be careful to avoid smudging the images before they have dried.

STEP 10 When you have completed all of the stamping, either rub out the pencil marks or paint over them using the small artist's brush and a little of the white emulsion paint.

Breakfast-

Elevenses-

Dinner- Tea-

Midnight Snack-

Enlarge or reduce this template to suit the size of the project.

CHAPTER 7

SIMPLE
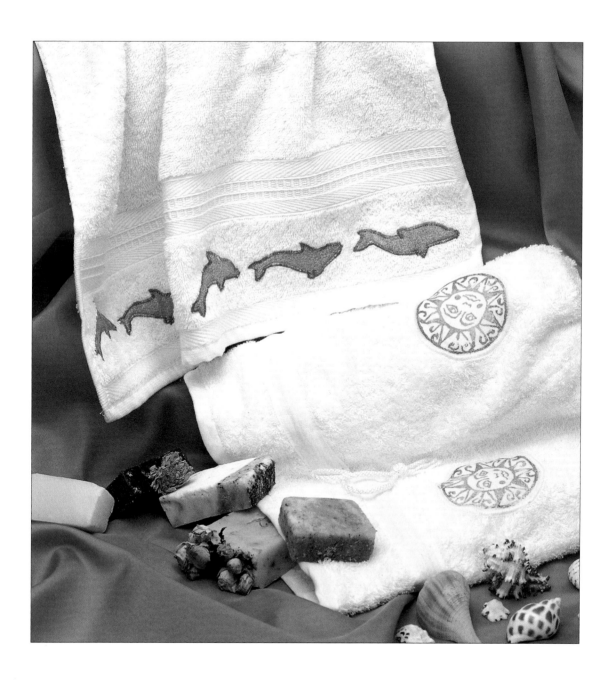
APPLIQUÉ

Technique

Appliqué is the art of sewing a fabric motif on top of another piece of fabric. It is great for re-vamping all manner of household items, from bed linen to old clothes. Most people use a sewing machine that can produce a zigzag stitch, but a simple hand stitch will work just as well.

Materials *and equipment*

- Needles
- Thread
- Pins
- Scissors (large and small)
- Sewing machine that can produce a zigzag stitch
- Fabric motif to be appliquéd
- Item to be decorated
- Circular sewing frame (optional)
- Thimble
- Tailor's chalk
- Tape measure

Method

STEP 1 Before attaching any fabric motif to your chosen item ensure that neither will shrink in the wash.

STEP 2 Cut roughly around your motif, leaving a margin of at least 2.5cm (1in) around the design.

STEP 3 Pin the motif into place, then carefully tack inside the stitching line so that the fabric cannot move while you are stitching. To make it easier, mount the item into the sewing frame. If you do not have one just use more tacking stitches. The frame is just to keep the fabric item tight.

STEP 4 Set your machine to zigzag stitch, with a stitch length of between 0.2 and 0.4 and a stitch width of approximately 4. Carefully stitch around the outside of the design, following its line as closely as possible.

STEP 5 Tie off all the loose ends on the underside the fabric.

STEP 6 Using the small scissors, carefully cut away the excess fabric outside the zigzag stitch. Lift the fabric you are cutting away from the material below to avoid damaging the latter. Use small, careful snips and work slowly around the design.

STEP 7 Once you have cut away all of the excess fabric, remove all of the tacking threads carefully.

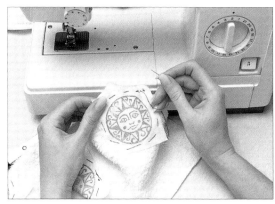

Step 3

Step 4

Step 6

⬖ *Tips*

- Tack using a cotton of a contrasting colour so that it is easier to
  see the stitches when you come to remove them.

- If you wish to save time and avoid tacking, stick the design into
  place with heat-activated iron-on bonding fabric. This is available
  from most good fabric/haberdashery shops.

- Pull loose threads through to the back of the item to tie them
  off. This is neater and improves the loof of the finished piece.

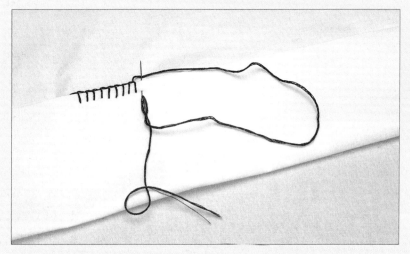

⬖ *Blanket stitch*

- If you do not have a sewing machine, you can appliqué using
  a hand stitch such as blanket stitch.

- If your fabric is likely to fray in the wash, finish the edges
  in some way, with a machine zig-zag for example.

Dolphin hand towel

Make this fun towel using a lively stamp of three swimming dolphins. If you really want to go to town, why not give the whole bathroom a face-lift? You could use this technique to make yourself a complete set of towels and face flannels.

- Needles
- Coloured tacking cotton
- Blue thread
- Pins
- Scissors (large and small)
- Sewing machine that can produce a zigzag stitch
- Fabric for the motif (white cotton or medium-weight calico)
- Dolphin group palette stamp by CaroLines (catalogue no: 10C39K)
- Blue Fabrico ink pad
- Iron
- White towel
- Thimble

Materials **and equipment**

Method

STEP 1 Wash all the fabric and allow it to dry naturally.

STEP 2 Stamp the correct number of images onto the fabric that you are using for the motif. It is easier to stamp all three dolphins in each motif now and trim the ones you do not want later. Ensure that there is at least 5cm (2in) between each trio of dolphins. Set the ink as detailed in the manufacturer's instructions.

Step 2

STEP 3 Cut out the motifs, ensuring that at least 2.5cm (1in) of fabric remains around each one.

STEP 4 Pin your motifs into place and tack them carefully inside the stitching line to ensure that they do not move when you are machine stitching. Make sure that you keep your design coherent by tacking down the correct dolphin. If you wish, you could use the whole image and just appliqué it once to the corner of the towel.

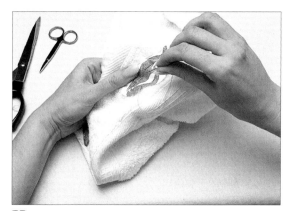

Step 4

STEP 5 Using the blue thread and a broad, short zigzag stitch (length 0.2–0.4, width approximately 4) sew around your selected dolphins, tie off all the ends of cotton on the reverse of the towel and cut away the excess fabric left outside the stitching.

STEP 6 Remove all tacking stitches and iron the completed towel thoroughly.

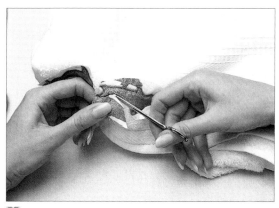

Step 5

PROJECT 2

Toiletries bag

This little bag is great for taking away with you and ensuring that you have a safe place to put all your toiletries. It is quick and easy to make and you can easily adapt the colours to suit your taste or match the towels and decor of your own bathroom.

Materials
and equipment

- Needles
- Cream cotton thread
- Coloured tacking cotton
- Pins
- Scissors (large and small)
- Sewing machine that can produce zigzag stitch
- Cream terry towelling (30 x 90cm (12in x 1yd))
- Plastic lining (30 x 90cm (12in x 1yd))
- Medium-weight calico (10 x 40cm (4 x 16in))
- 1.5m x 2.5cm (1½yd x 1in) cream bias binding
- Cream cord (2m (2yd))
- Poppy red Fabrico stamp pad
- Tangerine Fabrico stamp pad
- Small artist's brush
- Sun stamp by The Stamp Connection
  (catalogue no: H7229)
- Thimble

Method

STEP 1 Prewash the fabric.

STEP 2 Cut a rectangle 67 x 28cm (26½ x 11¼in) and a circle 20cm (8in) in diameter from the terry towelling. Cut out the same sized pieces from the plastic.

STEP 3 Paint the two Fabrico inks onto the sun stamp: use the tangerine for the centre and the poppy red for the outer rim, then stamp four images onto the medium-weight calico. Set the ink as specified in the manufacturer's instructions.

STEP 4 Cut out the stamped designs, leaving at least 2.5cm (1in) around the edge.

STEP 5 Neaten the edges of the terry towelling with either an overlocking or a zigzag stitch.

STEP 6 Pin the sun images onto the terry towelling rectangle and tack them securely into place. Make sure that they are not placed within the seam allowance.

STEP 7 Using a wide, short zigzag stitch (length 0.2–0.4, width approximately 4) stitch around each of the sun images. Knot off all loose threads on the reverse.

STEP 8 Carefully cut any excess fabric away, ensuring you do not snip the zigzag sewing and the fabric itself.

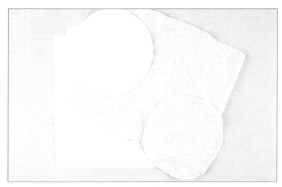

Step 2

Step 4

STEP 9 Cut two pieces of bias binding 29cm (11½in) long. The cord will be threaded under these to draw the neck of the bag together. Turn over each end of both bias strips approximately 6mm (¼in), sew them down and knot off the threads. Spread the rectangular piece of terry towelling flat on your work surface. Lay the two pieces of bias binding parallel to the top of the bag 5.5cm (2½in) away from the edge, leaving a gap of 2cm (¾in) between them. Pin, tack and sew them into place, leaving the ends unsewn.

Step 9

Step 13

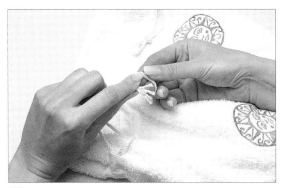

Step 15

STEP 10 Fold the terry towelling rectangle in half, with the right sides together, so that the two shorter edges meet. Using a 1.5cm (½in) seam allowance, pin, tack and sew down the rectangle so that it becomes a tube.

STEP 11 Carefully pin the circular piece of terry towelling into the base of the bag (opposite end to the bias binding). Tack and sew it into place with a seam allowance of 1.5cm (½in). Turn the bag right way out.

STEP 12 Make the lining in exactly the same way (follow steps 10 and 11).

STEP 13 Leave the lining the wrong way out, and place it inside the towelling bag. Bind over the top of the bag with the remaining bias binding, ensuring that the outer bag and inner lining are both caught into the stitches. In this way all rough edges will be hidden inside the bag or covered with bias binding. If you find it hard to sew through all three layers, sew the towelling and the plastic first and then attach the binding.

STEP 14 Cut the cord in half and thread each piece through one of the open-ended bias binding strips.

STEP 15 Knot off the cord to complete the bag.

CHAPTER 8

GLASS PAINTING

Technique

Glass painting is one of many craft techniques that have undergone a revival and, with new products coming onto the market each day, the glass painter's choice has never been so good. Even if you cannot draw, or have never painted before, mixing this craft with rubber stamping will enable you to create a wide range of attractive items. It offers the opportunity not only to recycle and re-vamp jam jars, bottle and other glass items you may have around the home, but to create beautiful cards as well.

When combining rubber stamping with glass painting you remove the need for the outliner, which is the most difficult part of modern glass painting to master. Using a suitable stamp, which provides large bold areas to paint, will enable all those of us who cannot draw a chance to create something really special.

Materials
and equipment

- Acetate film (use the type suitable for the photocopier as this will not curl when heated)
- Rubber stamp
- Black pigment ink
- Embossing powder (for beginners, I suggest black)
- Heat source (embossing heat gun, paint stripper or toaster)
- Glass paints (various colours)
- Man-made sponge (for example a washing-up sponge)
- Small palette
- Small artist's brush
- Shallow plastic tray
- Rubber gloves
- Newspaper (to cover the work surface)
- Fluid to clean brushes (as per manufacturer's instructions)
- Small pot (to hold cleaning fluid)
- Cotton buds (to correct smudges and spills)
- Toothpick

Method

In the following projects I have used acetate film and mirror glass to demonstrate the stamping, embossing and glass painting techniques, because I have found that it is easier for the beginner to start with a flat surface. With a little practice, the beginner will gain confidence and be able to move onto curved surfaces, such as bottles or vases – there is no end to the glass items you can decorate once you have mastered these techniques.

STEP 1 Ink the rubber stamp thoroughly with the ink pad and stamp onto the acetate. Try not to rock the stamp, and lift it off vertically to avoid smudges.

STEP 2 Sprinkle the image with embossing powder and remove the excess. Embossing powder will stick to finger marks and static, so blow gently to remove any stubborn powder, or use a small brush.

STEP 3 Now heat the powder. Move the heat source continuously over the image and do not bring it too close to the surface.

STEP 4 Lay the acetate on a flat surface immediately after heating to ensure that it cools flat. Allow it to cool before you handle it.

Step 4

Techniques

APPLYING A SMOOTH COAT OF COLOUR

Dip the brush into the paint, loading it heavily to cut down on bubbles and push or drag the paint rather than using a normal 'painting' technique. If the amount on the brush does not cover the area, pick up more paint and add it to the pool of colour already on the acetate. Glass paints show brush strokes far more than other paints, so when using a large amount of paint on a flat surface, let the paint find its own level and the brush strokes will disappear. However, take care when working on a curved surface not to use too much paint as it will run to the lowest point and such areas will be covered more thickly than others.

 The ordinary painting technique

SPONGING

Sponging creates a textured finish and can be used to cover any blemishes. Pour some glass paint into a small palette, dip a sponge into it and gently dab the colour. Do not put too much paint onto the sponge as the paint will try to even itself out. Do not dab too vigorously or you might introduce air bubbles. You can burst them with a toothpick or see how they look when they are dry.

 Sponging

STIPPLING

Stippling offers more control than sponging and is used to create a textured finish. It is ideal for creating the look of fur. Paint the image in the normal way and allow the paint to become tacky. At this point, break the surface of the paint by dabbing a clean, dry brush up and down on the surface. If the paint is still too wet then it will smooth itself out again, so wait a few minutes longer and try again.

 Stippling

Wet-on-wet

Wet-on-dry

Speckling

WET-ON-WET

This method of mixing two colours does not offer you much control over the final outcome, but can create interesting effects when you are painting natural images where straight lines look out of place, on petals for example. Apply one paint in the normal manner then, while the paint is still wet, apply a second colour over the top. You will find that the two colours start to move inside each other creating subtle changes. This method can also be used to create a soft blend between adjacent colours. Apply one colour then a second colour next to it while the first is still wet. Where the colours meet they will merge rather than give you a solid line. When using this technique it is best to start with the lighter colour and then add the darker colour.

WET-ON-DRY

This technique gives you more control over the finished effect, but does not provide the fluid movement that can be achieved with the wet-on-wet technique. Start with the lighter colour. Paint the image in the normal manner and allow to dr completely, then apply your second colour over the first.

SPECKLING

Speckling is a great technique for adding further interest to your image but, again, you have little control over the effect. Paint the image in the normal manner and, while the paint is still wet, drop some white spirit (or other cleaning fluid) onto the surface of the paint. The white spirit will take away a little of the colour, leaving areas which are almost bleached in appearance.

MARBLING

This technique can only be
produced with solvent-based paints,
and you will be unable to control
the result because the paints are
moving continuously. Fill a plastic
tray with water and drop your
selection of colours onto the surface
where they will float. To mix the
colours, blow gently on the surface
of the water. Once you are happy
with the pattern, place the item to
be marbled into the water, then pull
it straight up and away. Put it to
one side to allow the paint to dry.
This takes a little longer than
normal. When marbling acetate,
just lower it until it comes into
contact with the surface of the
water and paint, then pull it
vertically away.

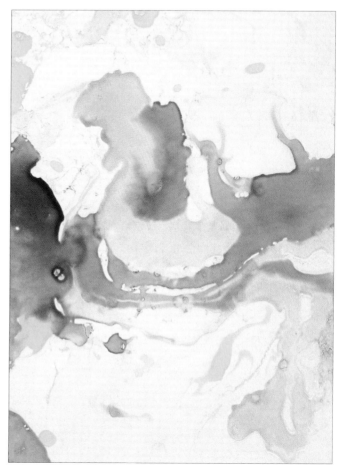

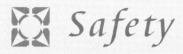 *Marbling*

⬥ *Safety*

- Some solvent-based paints can give off strong fumes, so always use them in a well-
  ventilated room. If you find yourself becoming light-headed, open the windows and get
  some fresh air. Always ensure that the paints and cleaning fluids are kept in a safe
  place, and always read the instructions before using a new type of paint.

 *Tips*

- Press stamp down harder than usual to ensure a clean, bold image.

- When stamping onto a curved surface it is sometimes easier to place the inked stamp face-up on the work surface and slowly roll the item over it.

- Carry out a small trial first to see if the paints react with the embossing powder. If you find that the embossing powder rises from the surface, then paint on the reverse side of the glass or acetate so that the two do not touch one another, or alter the make of paints you are using (this can be a question of trial and error). Obviously, painting on the reverse is not always possible. You will have to experiment to find an embossing powder and paint which do not react.

- I have found that some makes of paints will not allow you to carry out the wet-on-dry technique. When you put the second colour over the first it blisters and pulls away from the acetate or glass surface. Carry out a small trial first.

- If the area to be covered is large and bubbles or fluff spoil the surface then stipple the offending area to mask any blemishes.

- To reduce the risk of dust and fluff ruining an otherwise good piece of work, make yourself a drying box out of a large cardboard box that you can close while the paints dry.

- When working on a 3-D piece, keep it steady on an old sticky tape reel.

- When you wish to marble a large 3-D item, use a plastic bowl or bucket.

- When marbling, prevent the paint from coming into contact with the surface of the item a second time in the following way: slowly lower the item into the water and before you pull it back up, blow gently around the edge of it to push the paint back.

Bathroom mirror

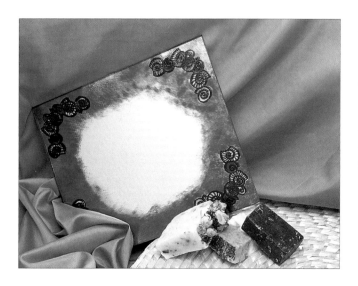

Add a little interest to a plain or boring mirror with this shell corner stamp and a few glass paints. All you need is a little time and a steady hand to create something new and original. The design can also be used on a variety of other items to create a whole new look for your bathroom.

- Mirror (25 x 20cm (10 x 8in))
- Shell corner rubber stamp by The Stamp Connection (catalogue no: H7016)
- Embossing ink
- Black embossing powder
- Heat source (embossing heat gun, etc)
- Fine artist's brush
- Glass paints (various colours)
- Suitable cleaning fluids
- Newspaper (to cover the work surface)
- White spirit
- Scrap paper
- Small sponge
- Small scissors

Materials
and equipment

Method

STEP 1 Clean the mirror with a little white spirit and allow it to dry.

STEP 2 Stamp one corner with the image and sprinkle the black embossing powder over the wet ink.

STEP 3 Heat the embossing powder in the normal way. Allow the mirror to cool before starting on the next corner, because it can get very hot. Print the other corners.

STEP 4 Carefully paint each shell with your chosen colour. It is easier if you work with one colour at a time and finish painting all the areas that require it before moving on to the next colour.

STEP 5 Ensure all the paints are dry. Stamp the image four times onto scrap paper and cut them out. Place these cut-outs over the painted corners to mask them while you sponge colour around the outer edge of the mirror.

Step 2

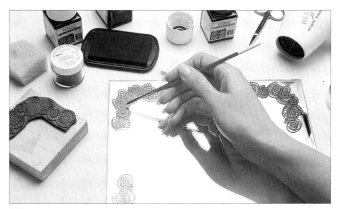

Step 4

Step 5

PROJECT 2

Framed image

Remember a happy moment in your life by framing a favourite image with an individual frame. It is easy to make and has the advantage that you can change the image as the years go by.

- Frame (17.5 x 12.5cm (7 x 5in))
- Rubber stamp by Creative Stamps (catalogue no: HH552K. Other versions of this stamp are also available)
- Embossing ink
- Black embossing powder
- Heat source (embossing heat gun, etc)
- Fine artist's brush
- Glass paints (various colours)
- Cleaner suitable for the paints used
- Newspaper (to cover your work surface)
- White spirit
- Small piece of rag or tissue
- Card to fit the picture frame
- Craft knife and cutting mat or scissors
- Piece of A5 paper
- Pen

Materials
and equipment

Method

STEP 1 Remove the glass from the frame and clean it with a little white spirit. Allow it to dry.

STEP 2 Ink the stamp with the embossing ink and stamp the image onto the glass.

STEP 3 Sprinkle with the black embossing powder and heat in the normal way. Allow the glass to cool, because it will get very hot.

STEP 4 When the glass is cool, carefully paint the image. Put the glass to one side and allow the paints to dry.

STEP 5 While the paints are drying, stamp the image onto the piece of paper and, when the ink is dry, cut out the centre section using the craft knife or scissors. This forms a template so that you can cut an aperture in the card.

STEP 6 Making sure that the aperture lines up with the stamped image, draw through the aperture in the paper onto the card. Now carefully cut the aperture out of the card.

STEP 7 Write your chosen message onto the card. If you are worried about making a mistake pencil the message in first.

STEP 8 Once the paint is dry, replace the glass, put the card behind it, and insert your picture in. To stop the photograph moving, use a little masking tape on the reverse to hold it in place.

STEP 9 Replace the back of the frame.

Step 2

Step 4

Step 6

Step 9

CHAPTER 9

PAINT EFFECTS

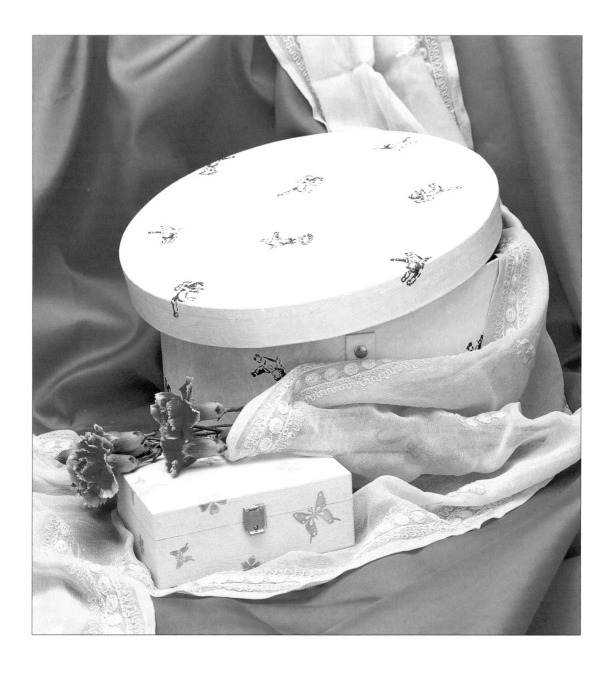

Technique

During the last few years the use of paint effects has grown and grown, to such an extent that there are now complete courses designed solely around different paint effects. All manner of special brushes and paints are available, alongside the more usual emulsion paints used to decorate walls and household items. New materials, equipment and techniques are emerging all the time. The tools used to create different paint effects can be as expensive or as cheap as you wish them to be, and this craft can be kept really basic by just using such items as old cotton sheeting or even an old shopping bag.

This chapter will cover just a few of the basic techniques and paint effects that can be used. I have kept the tools simple and cheap, so that the projects are kept within anyone's budget. Use this chapter as a stepping stone to other more complicated and more expensive paint effects. You will be amazed at the effects that can be achieved using simple household items. Don't be afraid to experiment freely; the only limit is your imagination, and with so many new products being introduced, your imagination is given a helping hand whenever it gets stuck for ideas.

Materials
and equipment

- Rubber gloves
- Scumble glaze or other specialist glazing medium
- Emulsion paints or specialist paint suitable for the glazing medium
- Natural sponge
- Cotton rag
- Stockingnet material
- Foam decorative stamps
- Plastic bag
- Bubble pack
- Scissors
- Decorating brush
- Item to decorate
- Newspaper (to cover the work surface)
- Masking tape

Method

For both of the following projects, the first thing you need to do is paint a base coat onto your chosen item. Paint the base coat in the colour of your choice (see Tips below) and allow it to dry. For better results, paint the base coat on to the blank item or wall with a roller. In this way you will avoid leaving unattractive brush marks.

SPONGING OFF

STEP 1 Mix the scumble glaze and the second paint colour as directed on the container. Paint a section of the item or wall (when working on walls, only paint this second layer in small areas, perhaps a metre at a time).

STEP 2 Dab the natural sponge onto the surface of the wet paint to remove some from the surface. Try to work randomly, so that a pattern does not form.

STEP 3 Work in this way until the item or wall is completely covered, and allow it to dry.

Sponge effect

Tips

- To sponge into the corners (which are the hardest areas to reach), tear off a small piece of sponge and gently tap into the corners.

- Only use a natural sponge; man-made sponges give too even a texture.

- When working on large areas, try to ensure that the sponge does not become too clogged with paint. If necessary, clean it at regular intervals by wiping it on paper.

RAGGING

STEP 1 Mix the glaze and the second paint colour according to the manufacturer's instructions and paint the second coat, again working in small areas, perhaps a metre at a time.

STEP 2 Take the rag and scrunch it into a ball, with lots of creases in its surface.

STEP 3 Dab the rag onto the surface of the wet paint and, as with the sponging off technique, it will remove some of the paint.

STEP 4 Work over the entire area trying to ensure that a regular pattern does not appear in the paint's surface.

STEP 5 Continue in this way until the wall or item is completely decorated.

Ragging effect

Tips

- Keep the edges of the rag turned in to ensure frayed cotton does not infiltrate the paint.
- Experiment with different fabrics to achieve different results.
- Ensure that you have plenty of rags cut to size (about 50cm (20in) square) to complete the project.
- Try to ensure that the fabric does not become too clogged with paint by regularly re-forming the ball so that dry parts come into contact with the glaze.

BAGGING

STEP 1 Mix the glaze and second paint colour as directed in the manufacturer's instructions, and paint the wall or item in small sections.

STEP 2 As with ragging, crumple the plastic bag into a ball, allowing a lot of creases to form.

STEP 3 While the second coat of paint is still wet, dab the area with the bag.

Bagging effect

📎 *Tips*

- Do not use the outside of the plastic bag if it has wording on it, as this might come off onto the item and ruin the paint effect.

- Change the bag regularly so that its surface does not become too clogged with paint.

BUBBLE-PACKING

STEP 1 Wrap the bubble pack around the natural sponge and brush a small amount of the second paint onto the surface of the bubble pack. This technique does not require the addition of glaze.

STEP 2 Remove excess paint by dabbing it onto a piece of newspaper.

Bubble-packing effect

STEP 3 Now dab the bubble pack onto the surface of the item or wall, with a little twist of the wrist. This should result in small swirling patterns in the surface of the paint.

STEP 4 Try to overlap some of the swirls and ensure that a pattern does not form by working randomly.

✂ *Tips*

- Experiment with different-sized bubble packs for different-sized swirls.

- Make sure you have plenty of bubble pack to hand. You will need to renew the bubble pack on a regular basis because some of the bubbles will burst while you work.

✂ *Clothing effect*

CLOTHING

STEP 1   When the base coat is dry, paint the second colour over the first, using a mixture of paint and scumble glaze.

STEP 2   Using a small piece of the stockingnet material rolled into a ball, dab the surface of the wet paint. As you dab and lift the stockingnet it will leave an imprint in the surface of the paint. Work randomly.

✂ *Tips*

- Change the stockingnet on a regular basis so that it does not hold too much paint.
- Make sure you have plenty of material cut so that you do not run out during the project.

✂ *Stamping into paint effects*

STAMPING INTO PAINT EFFECTS

STEP 1   Once the paint effect has been completed and while the paint is still wet, take the stamp of your choice and press it firmly into the paint. Remove the stamp, trying to ensure that you pull it straight out so that you do not smudge the design. The stamp will leave its impression in the surface of the paint.

 *Tips*

- Scumble glaze and specialist glazing media are used to slow the drying time of the paint, giving you time to create the desired effect. With some effects, such as sponging, I have found it possible to work without the glazing agent. Scumble glaze and similar glazing media are available from most good DIY stores and some good hobby/craft shops.

- Using silk emulsion or soft silk paints stops the glaze sinking into the base coat.

- When using two colours, start with a neutral colour (cream or ivory) as your base coat under a stronger colour. Avoid using brilliant white as your base coat as it will create a 'cold' feel to the finished paint effect. Mixing colours can be fun. Try using either two tones of the same colour (for example a light blue beneath a dark blue) or two completely different colours. When using two different colours, the top colour might change slightly because it will be affected by the base coat (for example, red under blue might make the completed effect purplish).

- The base coat should be either a vinyl silk or an eggshell paint.

- If your item is to be handled or will receive a lot of wear and tear, varnish it with a clear matt varnish when the paint is completely dry.

- To add interest to your paint effects, particularly less-textured ones, try stamping your favourite stamp on top while the paint is still wet.

PROJECT 1

Cupid hat box

Use the bubble pack paint technique to create a sky full of clouds for these lovely little cherubs to play in. This item is not only suitable for keeping summer hats safe and dust free, but will also double up as a great hiding place for those letters and notes we all keep. It is also decorative enough to be put on display on top of your wardrobe or in a corner of the bedroom.

- Scrap white paper
- Black ink pad
- Small scissors
- Plain hat box to decorate
- Light blue emulsion paint
- White emulsion paint
- Bubble pack and a small natural sponge
- Small household paintbrush
- Embossing ink pad
- Cupid rubber stamps by Clarity Stamps
- Artist's brush
- Dark blue embossing powder
- Heat source (embossing heat gun, etc)
- Varnish (suitable for the item being decorated)
- Suitable cleaning fluids
- Blu-tack
- Newspaper (to cover the work surface)

Materials *and equipment*

Method

STEP 1 Paint the hat box evenly with the light blue paint and allow to dry. If required, paint a second coat and allow it to dry completely.

STEP 2 Once it is dry you can add the white paint, using the bubble pack to create 'clouds' (see page 97). Allow the paint to dry.

STEP 3 While the paint is drying, stamp each image onto the white paper several times using the black ink. Cut roughly around the designs. To work out the positions of the cherubs, put a little blob of Blu-tack onto the back of each image and press it into place. Once you are happy with the positioning, work systematically from one side to the other stamping and embossing each cherub in turn.

STEP 4 To complete the hat box apply several coats of varnish. The more coats of varnish you apply the better the finish and the more hard-wearing the hat box will be.

Step 2

Step 3

PROJECT 2

Keepsake box

This lovely little hinged box is ideal for small keepsakes and will grace any dressing table. The sponging effect is quick and simple to do and the colours can be altered easily to match the decor of your own home. The butterflies add a simple finish which is sure to please the most discerning eye.

Materials
and equipment

- Small hinged box blank
- Fine-grade sandpaper
- Apple white emulsion paint (or similar)
- Light green emulsion paint
- Small household paintbrush
- Natural sponge
- Small paper scissors
- Blu-tack
- Scrap paper (to stamp on)
- Rubber stamps (CaroLines: 11C44C, 12C44A, 4C54A and 15C54A)
- Multicoloured ink pad
- Matt spray varnish
- Newspaper (to cover work surface)
- Masking tape

Method

STEP 1 Sand the box blank with the fine-grade sandpaper to ensure that any rough edges are removed.

STEP 2 Mask off the catch and the hinges of the box with a little masking tape.

STEP 3 Paint the box with at least two coats of the apple white emulsion paint.

STEP 4 When the base coat is completely dry, gently sponge the darker colour over the entire surface of the box using the natural sponge (see page 95). Allow to dry completely.

STEP 5 Stamp each image several times onto the scrap paper and cut them out roughly. Work out the position of each image and gently stick them into place with the Blu-tack.

STEP 6 Once you are happy with the position of each image, gently remove the cut-out and stamp the same image in that position. Stamp the rest of the images.

STEP 7 Allow the ink to dry, then varnish the whole box with several coats of matt spray varnish.

STEP 8 Remove the masking tape and remove any paint which may have strayed onto the hinges and lock.

Step 4

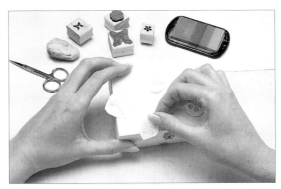

Step 5

Step 6

CHAPTER 10

PAINTING
CERAMICS

Technique

Painting on ceramics is far easier than you might think and with the introduction of new and varied products the crafter's choices are opening up all the time. Paints that harden in the ordinary kitchen oven are now available, meaning that you can achieve greater durability without a specialist oven.

Many of the products being introduced onto the market are relatively cheap and easy to use. Manufacturers are making them safe and easy to clean up. The colours available in some ranges may seem a little limited on first inspection, but you may find that they will mix, which opens up a whole spectrum of colours. The joy of this craft lies in the opportunity to decorate plain ceramic items and co-ordinate them with your home. Each piece can be made individual not only to the maker, but also to the room in which it is to live.

You can experiment with colours, shades and shapes. If you make a mistake and you are using water-based ceramic paints on washable ceramics, you can simply wash the paint off before it dries and try again. The golden rule is to remember that there are no such things as failures or things that go wrong, only experiments.

Materials
and equipment

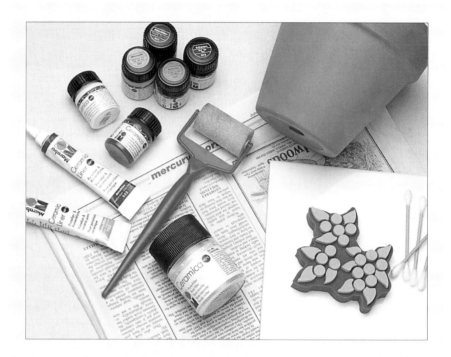

- Pore sealer (if necessary)
- Ceramic paints, such as Ceramica (in a variety of colours)
- Ceramic plate or tile, or plastic-coated paper plate
  (to hold your paint)
- Liquid ceramic liner
- Newspaper (to cover your work surface)
- Ceramic item to decorate
- Oven (if your paints require heat-fixing)
- Foam decorative stamps
- Foam roller
- Cotton buds (for mistakes and spills)

Method

STEP 1   Before you start to decorate your chosen item, you must wash it in warm soapy water and then allow it to dry completely.

STEP 2   Put a little of the paint you are using onto the plate. Take the roller and cover it evenly with the paint.

STEP 3   Use the roller to put an even coat of paint onto the surface of the foam stamp. Make sure you do not put too much paint onto the surface.

Step 3

STEP 4   Press the stamp firmly onto the surface of the ceramic item, trying to ensure that the whole stamp comes into contact with the ceramic surface.

STEP 5   Pull the stamp away from the item vertically in order not to smudge the image.

Step 5

STEP 6   Once the image is complete and the paints have had time to air dry (follow the manufacturer's instructions) place the item in the oven and bake as required.

⬚ *Tips*

- Try not to put too much paint onto the stamp or it will slip when you press it into place.

- If you do not have a sponge roller, use a medium-sized artist's brush to apply the paint.

- Experiment with placing different colours next to each other on the stamp to create some interest.

- If you have difficulty placing the stamp onto an item with a curved surface, put the stamp face up on a flat surface and roll the item across the stamp.

- Foam decorative stamps work better for ceramic paints than rubber stamps.

- Add interest to your design by using liquid liner. This comes in a tube and is available in various colours.

- If the item you are making is likely to get splashed or will need cleaning, ensure that you choose paints that are water resistant once fixed in the oven.

- If you want to paint onto a porous surface, for example on a ceramic plant pot, you must seal it with a pore sealer prior to painting.

PROJECT 1

Tiles

These tiles will cheer up any bathroom. You can use them free standing, in a frame, or on the walls interspersed among ordinary tiles. They are simple to make and the colour scheme can easily be adapted to suit your own decor. All you need in addition to the basic equipment is a little time and a steady hand. The paints used are water-based, but are waterproof once oven baked so they can be used for a variety of items. Have fun creating your own style with items that match throughout the room.

- Plain white ceramic tiles (15 x 15cm (6 x 6in))
- Yellow Ceramica paint
- Blue Ceramica liner
- Small foam roller (or a medium-sized artist's brush)
- Variety of foam stamps with aquatic motifs
- Cloth
- Plastic-coated plate or spare tile (to hold paint)
- Newspaper (to cover the work surface)
- Oven

Materials *and equipment*

Method

STEP 1   Ensure that the tiles are clean and free of dirt and grease by washing them in warm, soapy water. Allow them to dry.

STEP 2   Using the brush or the foam roller, load the first stamp with the yellow paint, ensuring a good even coverage over the whole of the stamp.

STEP 3   Stamp the design into the centre of the tile, taking care that the stamp does not slip when in contact with the tile.

STEP 4   Outline the stamped design and add little details, such as the eye and the bubbles, with the blue ceramic liner.

STEP 5   Following the manufacturer's instructions, allow the paint to air dry then bake the tiles in the oven for the required amount of time. Once this time has elapsed, turn off the oven and allow the tiles to cool slowly. Do not move them until they have cooled down.

Step 2

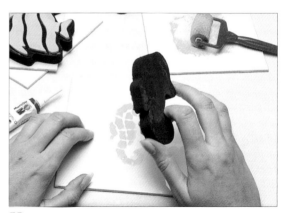

Step 3

Step 4

Tips

- Create a bubble stencil with a hole-punch; the bubbles can easily be stencilled by applying ceramic liner with a small sponge.

- If you are worried about smudging the stamped image while you are outlining, then allow the image to dry before you continue.

- If you make a mistake, for example, if you slip when stamping, wash the paint off while it is still wet and start again.

- Correct any small mistakes with a damp cotton bud. Just gently rub the error before the paint dries and it will come off easily.

- The design can be enhanced by using a tile that has a splashed water effect or some other simple, glazed design.

PROJECT 2

Pots

These ceramic pots are both functional and decorative, and you can use them for a variety of purposes, including displaying silk or dried flowers. You could even use them to house candles for your garden in summer. The simple ivy-leaf motif can be changed to suit your own taste and mood. If you like, you can add interest by applying liner which is available in various colours.

- Three ceramic garden pots (13, 16 and 19cm (5, 6½ and 7¾in) in diameter)
- Ceramica pore filler
- Green Ceramica paint
- Small foam roller (or medium-sized artist's brush)
- Medium household paintbrush
- Ivy-leaf foam stamp
- Cloth
- Plastic-coated plate or ceramic tile (to hold paint)
- Newspaper (to cover the work surface)
- Oven

Materials and equipment

Method

STEP 1   Remove any labels and ensure the pots are clean and free of dirt and grease by washing them in warm, soapy water. Allow them to dry completely.

STEP 2   Using the household paintbrush, cover the pots with an even coat the pore filler, which will serve as a primer for the paint. Sealing the surface in this way makes it easier to stamp the design later. Allow to dry completely.

Step 2

STEP 3   Put a little of the green paint onto the plastic plate or ceramic tile and roll the foam roller through it until it is loaded, then cover the foam stamp evenly with the paint.

STEP 4   Stamp the design onto each pot, rolling the stamp carefully around the body of the pots. The 16 and 13cm (6½ and 5in) pots will require one row of the stamp design, while the 19cm (7¾in) pot will require two.

Step 4

STEP 5   To add further interest, colour the pot-rims using the sponge roller and green paint. Allow the paint to air dry for approximately three to four hours.

STEP 6   Following the manufacturer's instructions, place the pots in the oven at the correct temperature for the required time.

Step 5

Tips

- If you choose larger pots, ensure that they will fit into your oven for 'baking'.
- Experiment with colour to create interesting effects. Put two colours onto the stamp with a brush and they will blend easily.

SUPPLIERS

AND MAIL ORDER SERVICES

ARTS ENCAUSTIC
Trem Ar Daf
Glogue
Pembrokeshire SA36 0ED

Tel: 01239 831401
Fax: 01239 831767

(Mail order service for all encaustic supplies, including stamps, waxes and sealer)

CAROLINES
42 Elm Hall Drive
Liverpool L18 5HZ

Tel: 0151 475 0667

(Mail order service for own range of stamps and stocks pre-cut frames)

CLARITY STAMPS
Ludwells Farm
Spode Lane
Cowden
Edenbridge
Kent TN8 7HN

Tel: 01342 850111

(Mail order service for own range of stamps, some specially designed for this book)

CREATIVE STAMPING
115 Stamford Road
Kettering
Northamptonshire NN16 8QZ

Tel: 01536 81778
Fax: 01536 521412

(Mail order service for stamps; own showroom and organisers of stamp/craft shows)

CRAFT CREATIONS
Ingersoll House
Delamare Road
Cheshunt
Hertfordshire EN8 9ND

(Mail order service for the aperture and pre-folded cards used in this book, plus other craft materials. Showroom open weekdays only)

EDDING UK LTD
Merlin Centre
Acrewood Way
St Albans
Hertfordshire AL4 0JY

Tel: 01727 846688

(Supplies paints and outliner)

**HARVEY BAKER
DESIGNS LTD**
Unit 1
Rodgers Industrial Estate
Yalberton Road
Paignton
Devon TQ4 7PJ

Tel: 01803 521515

(Mail order service for own wooden blank products)

**OPITEC EDUCATIONAL
MATERIALS LTD**
7 West Road
Woolston
Southampton
Hampshire SO19 9AH

Tel: 01703 446515
Fax: 01703 446991

(Mail order service for craft supplies, including wooden blanks)

PERSONAL IMPRESSIONS
E.M. Richford Ltd
Chilton Industrial Estate
Curzon Road
Sudbury
Suffolk CO10 6XW

Tel: 01787 375241

(Supplies selection of stamps)

P AND Q
Oak Tree Cottage
Evesbatch
Bishop's Frome
Worcestershire WR6 5BE

Tel/Fax: 01531 640001

(Mail order for stencil items and attend larger craft/hobby shows)

RUBBER STAMPEDE
Unit 9
Ashburton Industrial Estate
Ross-on-Wye
Herefordshire HR9 7BW

Tel: 01989 768988

(Supplies selection of stamps)

S FOR STAMPS
15 Southcroft Road
Glasgow G73 1SP

Tel: 0141 613 2680
Fax: 0141 613 2068

(Mail order service for stamps)

STONECRAFT®
Humatt Ltd
41 Shirley Street
London E16 1HU

Tel: 0171 474 6411

(StoneCraft® is the registered trademark of Humatt Ltd)

THE STAMP CONNECTION
4 Edith Road
Faversham
Kent ME13 8SD

Tel/Fax: 01795 531860

(Mail order service for own range of stamps)

Note: Copyright of all stamps is owned by the companies as cited for supply in the above listing.

ABOUT THE AUTHOR

Lynne Garner has been working at Harlow College for nearly four years, teaching a range of subjects including clothes making, interior design, paper crafts, candlemaking and glass painting to a wide range of students of all abilities.

She has been writing the rubber stamping and review columns for *Popular Crafts* since June 1997 and is adding other crafts, such as stencilling and candle making, to her work for this magazine.

In 1998, Lynne started to write the rubber stamping and review sections for the GMC craft magazine *Creative Crafts for the Home*, creating new projects each month based upon rubber stamping.

Lynne also designs her own stamps and has been working on some designs that are now in production and being sold by The Stamp Connection. The designs are based upon the cave paintings in the Ardèche region of France and Egyptian hieroglyphs.

Her spare time is spent with her fiancé, Jon, their 'set-in-her-ways' dog and a selection of sick and orphaned hedgehogs.

INDEX

TITLES AVAILABLE FROM

GMC Publications

BOOKS

WOODCARVING

The Art of the Woodcarver	*GMC Publications*
Carving Birds & Beasts	*GMC Publications*
Carving on Turning	*Chris Pye*
Carving Realistic Birds	*David Tippey*
Decorative Woodcarving	*Jeremy Williams*
Essential Tips for Woodcarvers	*GMC Publications*
Essential Woodcarving Techniques	*Dick Onians*
Further Useful Tips for Woodcarvers	*GMC Publications*
Lettercarving in Wood: A Practical Course	*Chris Pye*
Power Tools for Woodcarving	*David Tippey*
Practical Tips for Turners & Carvers	*GMC Publications*
Relief Carving in Wood: A Practical Introduction	*Chris Pye*
Understanding Woodcarving	*GMC Publications*
Understanding Woodcarving in the Round	*GMC Publications*
Useful Techniques for Woodcarvers	*GMC Publications*
Wildfowl Carving – Volume 1	*Jim Pearce*
Wildfowl Carving – Volume 2	*Jim Pearce*
The Woodcarvers	*GMC Publications*
Woodcarving: A Complete Course	*Ron Butterfield*
Woodcarving: A Foundation Course	*Zoë Gertner*
Woodcarving for Beginners	*GMC Publications*
Woodcarving Tools & Equipment Test Reports	*GMC Publications*
Woodcarving Tools, Materials & Equipment	*Chris Pye*

WOODTURNING

Adventures in Woodturning	*David Springett*
Bert Marsh: Woodturner	*Bert Marsh*
Bill Jones' Notes from the Turning Shop	*Bill Jones*
Bill Jones' Further Notes from the Turning Shop	*Bill Jones*
Bowl Turning Techniques Masterclass	*Tony Boase*
Colouring Techniques for Woodturners	*Jan Sanders*
The Craftsman Woodturner	*Peter Child*
Decorative Techniques for Woodturners	*Hilary Bowen*
Essential Tips for Woodturners	*GMC Publications*
Faceplate Turning	*GMC Publications*
Fun at the Lathe	*R.C. Bell*
Further Useful Tips for Woodturners	*GMC Publications*
Illustrated Woodturning Techniques	*John Hunnex*
Intermediate Woodturning Projects	*GMC Publications*
Keith Rowley's Woodturning Projects	*Keith Rowley*
Make Money from Woodturning	*Ann & Bob Phillips*
Multi-Centre Woodturning	*Ray Hopper*
Pleasure and Profit from Woodturning	*Reg Sherwin*

WOODWORKING

Stickmaking Handbook   *Andrew Jones & Clive George*
Test Reports: *The Router and Furniture & Cabinetmaking*   *GMC Publications*
Veneering: A Complete Course   *Ian Hosker*
Woodfinishing Handbook (Practical Crafts)   *Ian Hosker*
Woodworking Plans and Projects   *GMC Publications*
Woodworking with the Router: Professional Router Techniques
any Woodworker can Use   *Bill Hylton & Fred Matlack*
The Workshop   *Jim Kingshott*

UPHOLSTERY

Seat Weaving (Practical Crafts)   *Ricky Holdstock*
The Upholsterer's Pocket Reference Book   *David James*
Upholstery: A Complete Course (Revised Edition)   *David James*
Upholstery Restoration   *David James*
Upholstery Techniques & Projects   *David James*

TOYMAKING

Designing & Making Wooden Toys   *Terry Kelly*
Fun to Make Wooden Toys & Games   *Jeff & Jennie Loader*
Making Board, Peg & Dice Games   *Jeff & Jennie Loader*
Making Wooden Toys & Games   *Jeff & Jennie Loader*
Restoring Rocking Horses   *Clive Green & Anthony Dew*
Scrollsaw Toy Projects   *Ivor Carlyle*
Scrollsaw Toys for All Ages   *Ivor Carlyle*
Wooden Toy Projects   *GMC Publications*

DOLLS' HOUSES AND MINIATURES

Architecture for Dolls' Houses   *Joyce Percival*
Beginners' Guide to the Dolls' House Hobby   *Jean Nisbett*
The Complete Dolls' House Book   *Jean Nisbett*
The Dolls' House 1/24 Scale: A Complete Introduction   *Jean Nisbett*
Dolls' House Accessories, Fixtures and Fittings   *Andrea Barham*
Dolls' House Bathrooms: Lots of Little Loos   *Patricia King*
Dolls' House Fireplaces and Stoves   *Patricia King*
Easy to Make Dolls' House Accessories   *Andrea Barham*
Heraldic Miniature Knights   *Peter Greenhill*
Make Your Own Dolls' House Furniture   *Maurice Harper*
Making Dolls' House Furniture   *Patricia King*
Making Georgian Dolls' Houses   *Derek Rowbottom*
Making Miniature Gardens   *Freida Gray*
Making Miniature Oriental Rugs & Carpets   *Meik & Ian McNaughton*
Making Period Dolls' House Accessories   *Andrea Barham*
Making Period Dolls' House Furniture   *Derek & Sheila Rowbottom*
Making Tudor Dolls' Houses   *Derek Rowbottom*
Making Unusual Miniatures   *Graham Spalding*
Making Victorian Dolls' House Furniture   *Patricia King*
Miniature Bobbin Lace   *Roz Snowden*
Miniature Embroidery for the Victorian Dolls' House   *Pamela Warner*
Miniature Embroidery for the Georgian Dolls' House   *Pamela Warner*
Miniature Needlepoint Carpets   *Janet Granger*
The Secrets of the Dolls' House Makers   *Jean Nisbett*

CRAFTS

HOME AND GARDEN

VIDEOS

MAGAZINES

WOODTURNING ◆ WOODCARVING
FURNITURE & CABINETMAKING
THE DOLLS' HOUSE MAGAZINE
CREATIVE CRAFTS FOR THE HOME
THE ROUTER ◆ THE SCROLLSAW
BUSINESSMATTERS ◆ WATER GARDENING

The above represents a full list of all titles currently published or scheduled to be published.
All are available direct from the Publishers or through bookshops, newsagents and specialist retailers.
To place an order, or to obtain a complete catalogue, contact:

GMC Publications, Castle Place, 166 High Street, Lewes, East Sussex BN7 1XU, United Kingdom
Tel: 01273 488005 Fax: 01273 478606
Orders by credit card are accepted